THE
IMMORTAL
PROFESSION

THE
IMMORTAL
PROFESSION

THE JOYS OF
TEACHING AND LEARNING

GILBERT
HIGHET

WEYBRIGHT AND TALLEY
NEW YORK

Weybright and Talley
750 Third Avenue
New York, New York 10017

Library of Congress Cataloging in Publication Data

Highet, Gilbert, 1906-
     The immortal profession.

     Includes index.
     1. Teaching.   I.   Title.
LB1025.2.H5   371.1'02   76–5515
ISBN 0–679–40130–X

To

My Pupils 1932–1972

PREFACE

The art of teaching is an inexhaustible theme. Twenty-five years ago I published a short book on it, which has surprised me by its success. It has been reprinted fourteen times in English, and has been translated into Arabic, Dutch, French, German, modern Greek, Hebrew, Hindi, Indonesian, Korean, Lao, Malay, Persian, Portuguese, Spanish, Thai, and Urdu. Touching and eagerly enquiring letters have come to me from readers in many of these language-regions as well as from the United States and Great Britain and Canada. Many of the letter writers urged me to bring out a companion volume. Deeply engaged in other work, I had no time to write a genuine sequel, following up all its themes. But I continued to think about teaching: I wrote essays and made speeches on special aspects of the subject. Now they are brought together into this volume: which carries with it my thanks to the friendly audiences who heard some of its chapters delivered in the living voice, and my good wishes to the readers who, in spite of recurrent discouragements, continue to practice, with genuine selflessness and devotion, the immortal profession of teaching.

G.H.

East Hampton, New York
December, 1975

ACKNOWLEDGMENTS

My thanks go to the following, who were kind enough to answer questions and to make creative suggestions: Dr. William Abel of East Hampton, Mr. Keith Highet, Professor Graham W. Irwin of Columbia, Mr. Charles L. Mee Jr., and Dean Cyril C. Richardson of the Union Theological Seminary, New York.

CONTENTS

THE
IMMORTAL
PROFESSION

THE
PLEASURES OF
LEARNING

Why is teaching often so difficult for the teachers? and why is learning nearly always so hard for the pupils? There are many reasons; but one certainly is that, as most schools are set up today in the Western world, learning is something *compulsory*. It is an Ought: even worse, a Must. And in the lands of freedom the young now sneer at the Oughts and evade or resist the Musts with all their energy. Consider the drug habit. Soft drugs taken by the young may well injure them no more than strong drink (although in different ways); but hard drugs will most certainly give them a few thrills for a few weeks and then destroy their minds and bodies as irrevocably as cancer. Most drug addicts know this; but they take hard drugs partly because others—their parents, the police, the community—say they *must not*. Apart from the physical excitement, there is the thrill of defying authority, and there is also the thrill (as in fast driving or Russian roulette) of flouting danger. If the young could be told, and could understand, that hard drugs are forbidden, not because the Power Structure wants to spoil their fun, but because hard drugs are poison, some of them might decide not to experiment. But as long as the young think of drugs as a secret paradise from which cold parents and cruel police arbitrarily exclude them, they will be tempted.

The first human couple lived in Paradise, where they could do anything they wanted, except eat the fruit of one particular tree. Almighty God forbade them to eat it, without giving them any reason except one, which turned out to be false.* According to Scripture, the serpent persuaded Eve and she convinced Adam to contravene God's orders; but surely our two ancestors, like so many of their descendants, enjoyed the pleasure of rebellion, of independence, of liberty.

Learning, then, is difficult and even repulsive for the young as long as it is a Have-to imposed on them by authority, enforced by regular hours and rigid discipline. This feeling often lasts all through a lifetime. A good friend of mine, when I brought out my last book, asked me how many I had written altogether. When I said: "Fourteen, I think, not counting the little juvenilia," she laughed, and answered: "I don't think my Doug has *read* fourteen books since he left school. They shoved *Ivanhoe* and *Silas Marner* down his throat so hard that he still gags when he looks at a bound volume full of print. He never reads anything but the *Wall Street Journal* and *Sports Illustrated.*" Yet her Doug is a capable

---

*"Thou shalt not eat of it: for in the day that thou eatest thereof thou shalt surely die." However, Adam lived on to the age of nine hundred and thirty. (Genesis 2:17 and 5:5.)

fellow with a lively and versatile mind. It was early compulsion which "froze the genial current of his soul." Too often, for too many of us, learning appears to be an imposition, a surrender of our own will power to external direction, indeed a sort of enslavement. This is a mistake. On the contrary, learning is a natural pleasure.* It is a pleasure inborn and instinctive, one of the earliest pleasures and one of the essential pleasures of the human race.

If we ever doubt this, we can settle our doubts by watching a child, a very small one, at an age too young to have had any mental habits implanted by training. There are some delightful motion pictures made by Dr. Gesell of Yale, showing little creatures who can barely talk, and who certainly could not walk fifty yards, investigating problems with all the zeal and excitement of an explorer, making discoveries with the passion and absorption of a dedicated scientist, and striving to satisfy their own innate curiosity not only with the same faculty of intelligence but with something of the same dogged will power that makes an Aristotle, an Edison, or an Einstein.† At the end of each successful investigation there comes over each tiny face—hitherto bent in perplexity and wrinkled with concentration—a smile of pure heartfelt pleasure. When Archimedes discovered the principle of specific gravity by observing his own

---

*"To learn is very pleasant, not only for philosophers, but for other men too, except that they enjoy it on a smaller scale" (Aristotle, *Poetics* 1448b13–15): stated more boldly in *Metaphysics* i.i: "All men by nature desire to learn."

†A. Gesell, *Atlas of Infant Behavior* (New Haven, 1934): note especially the tower building (pp. 322–323), the bell ringing (p. 481), and the cup and spoon experiment (p. 637).

displacement of water in a bathtub, he leapt out with delight, shouting *"Heureka, heureka!* I have found it, I have found it!" The instinct which prompted his outburst, and the rapture of its gratification, are possessed by all children: a deep, a natural pleasure.

But if the pleasure of learning is universal, why are there so many dull, incurious, stupid people in the world? It is because they were *made* dull, by bad teaching, by isolation, by surrender to routine; sometimes, too, by the pressure of hard work and poverty, which benumbs the minds of millions of poor farmers and drudges throughout the world; sometimes, again, by the toxin of riches, with all their artificial anxieties, their second-rate satisfactions, and their ephemeral and trivial delights. With luck and resolution and good guidance, however, the human mind can survive not only poverty, but even wealth.

This pleasure is obviously not confined to learning from textbooks, which are too often tedious and sometimes repellent. But, among other things, it does mean learning from books, from all books worth remembering and even from some which appear forgettable yet hook themselves onto one corner of the mind. Sometimes, when I stand in a big library like the Library of Congress, or Butler at Columbia, or Widener at Harvard, or Firestone at Princeton, and gaze round me at the millions of books, I feel a sober, earnest delight which is hard to convey except by a metaphor. These are not books, lumps of lifeless paper, but *minds* alive on the shelves. From each of them goes out its own voice, as inaudible as the streams of sound conveyed day and night by electric waves beyond the range of our physical hearing; and just as the touch of a button on our set will fill the room with music, so by taking down one of these volumes and opening it, one can call into range the voice of a man far distant in time and space, and hear him speaking to us, mind to mind, heart to heart.

But away beyond books, learning means keeping the mind open and active to receive all kinds of experience. One of the best-informed men I ever knew was a cowboy who rarely read a newspaper and never a book, but who had ridden many thousands of miles through one of the Western states. He knew his state as thoroughly as a surgeon knows the human body. He loved it. He understood it. Not a mountain, not a canyon, which had not much to tell him, not a change in the weather that he could not interpret. Such a man is as learned as any scientist, in his own special and almost equally difficult way. And so, among the pleasures of learning, we should include travel: travel with an open mind and an alert eye and a wish to understand other peoples, other places, rather than looking in them for a mirror image of oneself. If I were a young man now, I should resolve to see —no, to *learn*—all the fifty states of the Union before I was thirty-five years old. They are all different; and each of them is unimaginable until you visit it. There are dull and ugly patches in them all (even in California); and yet in all of them there are areas of extreme strangeness, that strangeness which is more memorable than all but the greatest beauty. At this moment I can call up from my memory bank a train winding slowly through an unspeakable desert without a tree or a blade of grass or a human habitation or a sign of life—the Bad Lands of South Dakota; a little village entirely inhabited by Negroes, half hidden among the strange trees of the Mississippi Delta; a lonely square, brightly lit by the noon-day sun and quite empty, in the middle of an Indian pueblo in New Mexico; friendly Italian-Americans inviting strangers to help them celebrate the decoration of St. Joseph's altar in New Orleans. This country is well worth learning.

Mountain climbing too is learning. Every new mountain one climbs is a fresh experience. It shows one a new aspect of nature, a new side of the relationship between earth and mankind, a new set of facts about oneself, and usually a new realm of physical beauty. Mountains differ, as symphonies and cathedrals do. The slender, sharp, brittle, treacherous Dolomites differ from the huge many-shouldered boulder-strewn masses such as Long's Peak in Colorado, just as a cactus differs from a giant sequoia, just as a hawk differs from a bear. Each is a work of God. Each is beautiful. Each is worth learning and loving, not without fear.

Learning also means learning to practice an art, or at least to appreciate an art. In middle age one's reflexes slow up and become dull. You can hardly learn to make sculpture really deftly or to play an instrument really skillfully if you start much after the age of thirty. Appreciation is possible at any age. But both practice and appreciation are easier when one starts young. Every new art you learn appears to you like a new window on the universe: it is like acquiring a new sense. I myself, because I was born and brought up in a hideous nineteenth-century industrial city, did not understand the slightest thing about architecture until I was in my twenties. Since then I have learned a little about the art, and it has been a constant delight to me. In my mind I have a permanent album containing bright pictures of the Blue Mosque in Istanbul, the little church of St. John Nepomuk in Munich, the exquisite acropolis of Lindos standing high above the shining Rhodian sea. Not only arts, but crafts are well worth exploring. A friend of mine took up bookbinding—without much enthusiasm—because his doctor ordered him to do something which would give him relaxation and activity without tension. It was difficult at first, and he found this a challenge. He gradually learned to square off the paper and the boards; to sew the pages; to fasten on the backstrip; and to maintain precision and neatness throughout. From that he went on to produce interesting designs for the covers of his newly bound books, first copying them from patterns, and then inventing them for himself. Within a few years he found that this simple and initially rather dull hobby had led him into fresh fields of enjoyment and appreciation. He began to collect fine books from the past five centuries of this small but refined craft; he developed an interest in the skills of printing; eventually he started a private press and had the joy of producing his own elegant books. Many other crafts there are: and most of them contain one essential pleasure, the pleasure of making something which will last and deserves to last.

As for *reading* books, that contains two different delights, both definable as learning. One is the pleasure of apprehending the unexpected: when one meets a new author who has a new vision of the world. It was a memorable experience for me when I first entered into the complex, sensitive, and distorted psyche of Marcel Proust; when I was first carried away on the enthralling surrealist fantasies of Ariosto, or struggled up toward heaven with the newly born gods of the Swiss epic poet

Spitteler. This pleasure can be renewed throughout life, whenever one meets a good new author from the present or from the past. But there is also the pleasure of deepening one's knowledge of a special field. For instance, one might enjoy reading about the Civil War, and then be drawn to one particularly moving part of it, the underground railway which carried escaping slaves northward to freedom. After reading two or three books on that early resistance movement one would be impelled to visit the chief way-stations, to drive along part of the route, and to reconstruct the lives and sufferings of those poor noble people, resolute organizers and thankful fugitives.

   Some people would judge such pleasures to be amusing but faint. They are mistaken—though most of them will never find it out—for three reasons. One is that, the more intense a pleasure is to begin with, the more rapidly and finally it disappears. This principle is the basis of the philosophical system called Epicureanism, which posits pleasure as the only basis of human action, but grades different pleasures very carefully according to their quotients of associated pain (like drug taking) or subsequent exhaustion (like extreme sexual activity), and places highest in its scale of motives the *durable* pleasures, which are necessarily the mildest and yet in the end the most satisfying. Another reason is that the more varied any pleasure is, the more lasting it will be. This disposes of Bentham's theory that, judged on the scale of pure enjoyment, pinball is as satisfying as poetry. People enjoy playing pinball (or pachinko, or fruit machines, those one-armed bandits), while other people enjoy listening to poetry and reading it and saying it to them-

selves. There is no way, therefore, of distinguishing between the pleasures of these different groups? All are
equal? True; except that the pleasures of pinball and
gambling die away into mechanical repetition or gloomy
pursuit of the unattainable. (Dostoievski at the gaming
table is like the drug addict waiting for his "fix" to take
effect for the five-hundredth time, and wondering whether he should try another injection and another and . . .)
But even if we live for ninety years we can never exhaust
the pleasures of poetry or art or music.

A third reason for choosing worthy occupations is
that, if we judge by the experiences of many men and
women of the past, men and women very different in
character and background, there is a great and sustained
pleasure to be found in learning. To imitate good models
is a fine way to live.

Once there was a soldier who was in an expeditionary
force fighting in the Balkans. (There is nearly always
fighting in the Balkans.) He was brave and energetic. His
comrades noted with astonishment that he paid no attention to the fierce cold of the winter and that when their
supplies were cut off he neither complained nor weak-
ened. This may have been because he was very tough
physically or because he had extra firm will power; but
perhaps it was really because he paid very little attention
to external things. When the other soldiers were not on
duty they gambled, or drank, or played games, or slept.
He used to think. Apparently he thought all the time. A
man who was in the same outfit told an extraordinary
story about how he loved thinking.

One morning he had an idea, and stood thinking
about it. There was some difficulty which he could

not solve. Instead of dropping the subject he stayed there and thought. When it got to midday men began to notice this, and told one another with surprise that ever since daybreak he had been standing there thinking. Finally, when evening came, some fellows in the outfit, after eating, took out their blankets and slept in the open, watching to see if he would stand there all night. He stood until dawn broke and daylight came: then he went away after saying a prayer to the sun.*

This eccentric soldier was the only member of that force whose name is remembered for good. He was Socrates. The job of thinking which he did then gave him all the pleasure of an exciting combat and all the absorption of a passionate emotional experience. When he said his prayer of thanksgiving to the sun, he was a happy man.

Many centuries later we meet someone with less of a gift for happiness. His diary shows that he had poor health all his life (unlike the robust Socrates) and many undeserved misfortunes—poverty, persecution, illness in his family, misuse of his talents by others. His parents had fled from their home during a religious pogrom, and he used to recall that his father taught him Greek as a little boy while they were hiding from their pursuers in a cave. Nevertheless he became one of the finest classical scholars of his age: his work is still profiting scholars four centuries after his death. He was really happy in only two activities: the contemplation of God and the study of his books. Here is a touching entry from his diary, for June 27, 1598:

------

*The story is put in the mouth of Alcibiades by Plato in *Symposium* 219e5–220d5.

All morning and all afternoon today I had to myself:
I was all my own. No one came to trouble me, except for an hour in the morning which a friend (no
friend to my studies) stole from me. For all the rest
of the time I paid my faithful duty to the divinities
of learning. O God, blessed be thy name for grant-
ing me this freedom.*

There, in the words of Isaac Casaubon, speaks the man
who is devoted to the pure pleasure of knowing and
learning.

In the eighteenth century there lived in southern England a quiet, country parson. He was neither as strong
as Socrates nor as learned as Casaubon. I suppose he
made a good vicar. But whereas most country parsons of
his time were apt to content themselves with their
weekly round of pastoral duties, together with some
hunting and some gossip and some port, this little fellow
did not. While still at school he had become interested in
nature and living things. Before he was sixteen he had
been noting down the regular arrivals of migratory
birds. So, when he settled down in his parish, he began
to keep a diary—not of his own adventures and mishaps,
but of something far more important, the manifold
changes and miracles taking place in the world of nature
around him. He watched the buds appearing, in a different rhythm for each kind of tree. He identified the cry
of birds, noting the exact day on which each was first
heard. He experimented with odd phenomena like the
fungoid growths called "fairy rings"; and as he rode
round his parish, year after year for forty years or so, he
built up a richly detailed account of its entire natural life.

---

*Ephemerides Isaaci Casauboni, ed. J. Russell, 1 (Oxford, 1850), 97.

This is Gilbert White's *Natural History of Selborne.** It shows us how a man with little money and scarcely any equipment can still, if he is interested and methodical, become a scholar and a scientist. (Such also was the poor French naturalist Jean-Henri Fabre, who produced ten volumes of marvelously acute observations of the world of the insects and the spiders, from work done mainly on his own small farm in southern France.) I should add that Gilbert White was not merely a scientific observer: he was something of an artist. Many of the descriptions in his book are as good as genre paintings by Constable or Corot. As we turn over the low-voiced pages, we see a herd of cows grazing in damp ground, while around them dive and swoop the wagtails, catching (White carefully notes the two different types of prey) both the flies that surround the sweating cows, and the larvae which their hooves turn up out of the moist earth. On the next page another picture shows us another instance of temporary symbiosis: a troop of horsemen rides across the Downs, accompanied by a troop of birds, as crows follow the moving plough.

Almost the greatest astronomer of the Greek and Roman world was Ptolemy of Alexandria. The tradition says that he lived peacefully in his observatory under the clear skies of northern Egypt for forty years, surrounded by his records and his discoveries. Many and great were his explorations of the starry universe: for instance, he described astronomical refraction in a way which was

---

*W. Johnson, *Gilbert White, Pioneer, Poet, and Stylist* (London, 1928); C.S. Emden, *Gilbert White in His Village* (New York, 1956); Gilbert White, *The Natural History of Selborne in the County of Southampton* (World's Classics no. 22, Oxford University Press, New York); A. Rye, *Gilbert White and His Selborne* (London, 1970).

not improved until Cassini, who lived fifteen hundred years later. Like many great men (for instance, Aristotle and Calvin) he wrote just one poem in all his life; but it expressed his whole life.

> Mortal I know I am, short-lived; and yet, whenever
>   I watch the multitude of swirling stars,
> then I no longer tread this earth, but rise to feast
>   with God, and enjoy the food of the immortals.*

Learning extends our lives (as Ptolemy said) into new dimensions. It is cumulative. Instead of diminishing every ten years or so, like health and strength, its returns go on increasing, provided . . .

Provided, first of all, that you choose a worthy subject. In Anatole France's *Crime of Sylvestre Bonnard* there is a Russian prince who has illimitable wealth, but can think of nothing better to do than to travel around the world collecting matchboxes; and an American intellectual prodigy who entered Harvard at the age of eleven ended up collecting streetcar transfers.† Almost anything can be made the subject of *some* kind of intellectual interest; but it is obvious that certain topics will never be important, and that others can have only a very minor grasp on the mind. A large subject like ESP or alchemy can spread out far; a small subject like the liturgy of the Armenian church will not. From time to time on TV one

---

Anthologia Palatina 9. 577; *Oxford Book of Greek Verse* no. 621.
†This was William James Sidis, on whom see an excellent study called "The Streetcar Named Paradise Lost," in Samuel Rosenberg's *The Come As You Are Masquerade Party* (Englewood Cliffs, N.J., 1970).

sees a short film devoted to *Curious Occupations*. Nearly always it is a somber warning against wasting our lives. The camera shows a lady who collects abalone shells and sorts them out until she finds some which look something like landscapes of the California shoreline; and then she carves them and adds bits to them and paints them until they look still more like landscapes of the California shoreline. By the time the camera crew reaches her she has spent thirty years making abalone shells into semblances of the California shoreline; and, judging by her face and voice, she has realized her mistake. That is the kind of error we must be careful to avoid.

Yet any choice involves a risk; and in any speculation you may lose. When I was about seventeen I decided to study all the piano works of Alexander Scriabin. I knew that he was believed to be a talented and original composer; that his later works were reputed to be almost unintelligible; that he had invented new basic chords and new harmonies which were somehow connected with a new mystical conception of life; and that both the music and the mysticism might be penetrated if approached slowly, stage by stage. So I bought Opus 1 and learned to play it, as far as I could; and then Opus 2, and so on. The music I found highly stimulating, although at first sometimes too imitative of Chopin and Liszt and sometimes pretty flimsy and superficial. Then, as I got further into it, I was disappointed to see that it was becoming far too difficult for any amateur to play. Scriabin himself was a superb pianist, and as his musical ideas developed he made his work far more complex and demanding, with cross rhythms and intricate figurations. And furthermore, the mystical side of the music

seemed—particularly during the arduous thirties and
forties of this century—far too other-worldly and guru-
ish: so that I turned back and pressed on no further,
although from time to time I still played some of the
earlier works. Was this all time and effort wasted? No.
Fifty years after I had first started exploring the music
of Scriabin without a guide, he was being programmed
at concerts, and entire record albums devoted to his music were appearing, performed by expert and sympathetic pianists, and his life and work were being intensively studied.* Now, although I know that the later
virtuoso pieces are forever beyond my own reach, I can
listen to them more intelligently because of my knowledge of the earlier works, which I still now and then
play, discreetly, after midnight.

First, then—even if it is a gamble—choose a worthy
subject or group of subjects to think about.

Second, your aim should be—throughout your life, as
you continue learning—to integrate your thought, to
make it complete, to make it harmonious. If you happen
to be an engineer and also to enjoy singing in a glee club,
then connect these two activities. They unite in you;
they are not in conflict. Both choral singing and engi-
neering are examples of the architectonic ability of man:
of his power to make a large plan and to convey it to
others who have never seen it, so clearly that they can
realize it and make it concrete. Both are aesthetic, one

---

*There is a good doctoral thesis, *The Nature and Development of
Scriabin's Pianistic Vocabulary*, which won the degree of Doctor of
Music for S.L. Randlett at Northwestern University in 1966; and a
new biography by Faubion Bowers, *Scriabin* (Kodansha International, Palo Alto, California, 1969).

openly and the other covertly. Both are more or less wordless, and depend much on symmetry, and are based on long experience and tradition; both are group activities; both are meant to produce or maintain something lasting. Think about the two together. If you do them, not as though they were quite dissociated but as though each were one aspect of a single unity, you will do them better, and be happier.

This is hard advice to give to young students. They are explosive. They are exploratory and insurrectionary and schizophrenic. I will not say that they are revolting; but they are rebellious. To integrate their lives, they find a task both difficult and repellent. They would rather seek outwards, and even try to move in opposite directions at the same time. The unhappiest and least successful people in the world are those whose conscious minds are fragmented, while their unconscious mentalities have grown into a firm, tight pattern and consolidated all their emotions. Reason is then dragged along, kicking and shouting, like a distracted rider who has been unseated by a powerful horse and still has one foot in the stirrup. Or sometimes the conscious mind remains in the saddle, swaying from side to side like a drunken cowboy, whooping and hollering in a false sense of freedom, while the steed itself gallops along on a desperate and doomed career.

Wholeness of the mind and spirit is not a quality conferred on us by nature or by God. It is like health, virtue, and knowledge. Man has the capacity to attain it; but to achieve it depends on his own efforts. It needs will power. It needs a long, deliberate effort of the mind and the emotions and even the body. Much unhappiness has been suffered by young men and women who have never

been taught, or have never accepted the principle, that
it is as desirable and as necessary to make themselves into
whole and harmonious personalities as to keep themselves clean and healthy and financially solvent. The
traveler through the Western world, as he moves from
one country to another, will often see an awkwardly
dressed youth or girl with a clumsy outward appearance,
yet bearing the unmistakable radiation of inner harmony; while soon afterward he will see a handsome
showily dressed youngster, with fine features, and yet
with a bitter, harsh discordance emanating, almost audi-
bly and almost visibly, from his or her poor tortured,
neglected mind. For the first, it will be comparatively
easy to learn good manners and poise; it will be terribly,
almost hopelessly, hard for the second to mold himself or
herself into a single unified and symmetrical personality.
The second aim, as one learns and goes on learning, is to
make oneself complete within oneself.

The third is the last and most important. This is based
on the unpleasant but central truth that, during our life
on this earth, the body gradually dies; even the emotions
become duller; but the mind in most of us continues to
live, and even grows more lively and active, enjoys itself
more, works and plays with more expansion and delight,
makes better discoveries and deeper investigations—all
this within a body which was once an arrogant and irrational master, but with age becomes a surly but half-
obedient servant. The long-range aim of our lives is
therefore to enjoy our physical being as long as possible;
but, knowing that this enjoyment will last only a short
period, say three or four hundred months, to build up
the longer-lasting and more reliable enjoyment of the

mind. When one of my own teachers, Gilbert Murray, became ninety years old, I was deputed by a classical society to send him felicitations and good wishes. In acknowledging the letter, he wrote: "I have a tendency to fall down unexpectedly from time to time, but my mind, thank God, is as good as ever."

This is not the dreary counsel which pious clergymen used to give in books with such names as *Holy Living and Holy Dying*: to prepare for death as though it might annihilate us at any moment. It is the wholesome advice to remember that a quick bet will not pay off so well as a long-term growth investment; to continue learning all through life exactly as one continues the practice of healthy habits of body. Many people have played themselves to death. Many people have eaten and drunk themselves to death. Nobody has ever thought himself to death. Thought is the only human activity which does not generate large quantities of harmful acids and alkalis. The chief danger confronting us is not age, or weariness. It is laziness, sloth, routine, stupidity, forcing their way in like wind through the shutters, seeping into the cellar like swamp water. Young people always think that they have all the hard temptations to face. But other temptations, less ardent but more persistent, will assail them later: the soft, sweet, cozy temptation of *laissez-faire*, the Sunday-morning-snooze temptation of casualness, the long-weekend temptation of triviality and temporariness. Many a brilliant mind, many a rich and powerful personality has fought its way through all the dangers, only to fall victim to the comforts. Both dangers and comforts are good for us; both can also be bad for us. Let us meet them both and beat them both.

The pleasures of learning are indeed pleasures. But in fact the word should be changed. The true name is happiness. There are three other types of happiness, superior to that of learning: the happiness of love fulfilled; the happiness of serving mankind; and the happiness of creation. Though it is beneath these, learning is still a great happiness, and can be a help toward the attainment of those others; and it is an essential part of a complete life. No learner has ever found that he ran short of subjects to explore. But many people who avoided learning, or abandoned it, find that life is drained dry. They spend thirty years in a club chair looking glumly out at the sand and the ocean; in a hotel lounge gossiping about the other inmates; in a porch swing waiting for somebody to drive down the road. But that is not how to live. The chief aim of education is to show you, *after* you make a livelihood, how to enjoy living; and you can live longest and best and most rewardingly by attaining and preserving the happiness of learning.

THE
ILLUSION OF
PROGRESS

In my young days I was devoted to science fiction—as who in youth is not? But in those times there was one science-fiction writer who consistently used good English. His name was H.G. Wells. I knew whole chapters of his work by heart. (Occasionally some of it approached poetry as closely as any such fantasies have ever done. The description in *The First Men in the Moon* of the rapidly advancing lunar sunset, through which the half-frozen moon explorer leaps and then stumbles and then crawls to reach his space vehicle before the atmosphere changes into airflakes and then into solid ice, is one of Wells's unforgettable pictures.)

When you read such things in youth, you are usually overcome by their imaginative scope. But it does not occur to you to question the moral assumptions behind them: so it took me some time to see through several of those on which Wells based his romances. (Also, he himself was highly sensitive and exceedingly versatile, so that he did not set out to preach a single moral doctrine which could be accepted or discarded as a unity.) One novel in particular long stayed in my mind as a lofty vision of the future, all mixed up with dreams and myths and archetypes. This was *The Food of the Gods* (1904). It told how a scientist invented a new food, which hugely accelerated the normal rate of growth in both animal and vegetable life. Rats that fed upon it grew to be as large as wild boars, wasps as big as barn owls; ordinary little water weeds soon choked the bed of a fair-sized river. The new food was given to a few human babies who were ailing and could not assimilate ordinary nourishment. The babies grew up into giants: handsome giants and beautiful giantesses they were, full of health and energy, towering about forty feet high and broad in proportion, something out of Wagner's *Ring*. The main conflict in the book was the struggle between the demands of the giants to be allowed to live by themselves and for themselves, even if it meant remolding part of our world to their needs, and the natural distrust and fear which ordinary people felt for them. No doubt Wells was translating Nietzsche's Superman into physical terms; also, he himself was undersized and puny, had been poor and downtrodden, and had made himself into an intellectual and imaginative giant. It was a good story.

Yet there was one huge falsehood in it. This was the assumption that all little people were usually mean and bad and that all big people were bound to be noble. In an idealistic speech one of the giants asks his fellows why they exist. He answers for them:

> To serve the spirit and the purpose that has been breathed into our lives. Tomorrow, whether we live

or die, growth will conquer through us. That is the
law of the spirit for evermore. To grow into greatness and the light. To grow and again—to grow.

With that the novel ends, on a picture of the superb
young monster pointing heavenward in a magnificent
pose of confidence and challenge.

This is a modern myth. Contrast it with the myths of
Greece and Rome and Judaea. There the giants are usually dangerous: the sons of Anak, who opposed the Israel-
ites invading Canaan; Goliath, the shaft of whose spear
was like a weaver's beam; the Cyclops, who was a brutal
cannibal (Odysseus says: "We saw him, and the sight
broke our hearts"); the earth-born Giants, savage and
snake-legged, who stormed heaven and tried to overthrow the Olympian gods. A few were kindly and heroic, such as Hercules and Samson; but very few.

Wells was writing a modern myth, using modern assumptions. One of those assumptions was that *power is
good.* A man of forty feet in height is bound (Wells
thought) to be noble and altruistic, whereas a man of five
foot six must be tormented by petty desires and fears and
weaknesses and a permanent sense of his own inadequacy. ("My little body," says Portia sadly, "is aweary of
this great world.") Yet that is not necessarily true. It may
be terribly false. Men forty feet high have more chance
of being devils than heroes. If we were all converted into
giants, each of us proportionately with as much strength
as twenty ordinary men, should we become, naturally
and logically, twenty times nobler than we now are?

To ask the question is to answer it. In writing this
myth, Wells laid hold of one vital fact about the human
psyche, and on that fact he built an edifice of imagination

which was brittle and false. The falsehood was the assumption that *power is good.* The vital psychical fact was that, for all mankind, *power is desirable.* Human beings are insatiable in their appetite for power, they cannot stop striving for it, it is an impetus implanted in them by their ancestry, which they can never eliminate and can only with difficulty bring under control. It is almost a reversal of the natural current of life for a man or woman with a big talent to refrain from using it; for someone who can make money to acquire only an adequate subsistence, and then stop; for a ruler of a country to give up all notion of extending his power both within and without his frontiers; for a man of our machine age to be content with his machines, never wishing to increase their speed, their horsepower, their total load, their complex and multiple activities. We live on a third-rate planet revolving around a fifth-rank star. But if the ambitions of humanity could control the tiny globe that is our home, we should long ago have converted it into a great orb of unprecedented size, roaring through the galaxy and trailing a long procession of asteroids; or perhaps blown it up altogether, providing temporary illumination and amusement for the rest of the cosmos.

Even the good giants in Greek and Hebrew myth found that their own strength made life harder for them. Samson became foolish; was captured, enslaved, and blinded; could not escape from servitude except by using his powers to destroy himself together with the enemies of the Lord. Hercules did mighty labors, killing ruffians and monsters, even once outfacing Death himself. But the tensions and excitements of his vast strength made it almost impossible for him to remain sane and balanced. He went mad and killed those whom he loved; finally the gift of a loving woman turned into a thing of endless torture, eating up his magnificent body, and he burned himself to death. Only then was he taken up into heaven and given the goddess of Youth to be his consort. In modern times it was Goya, with his thronging visions of the terrible, who best portrayed a giant. His painting "Colossus" shows a dun-colored plain bounded by low hills and a little forest. Across the plain stream crowds of people and animals, in great haste and distress—cattle running wild, a galloping horse throwing its rider, men and women rushing and stumbling in panic. Behind them an enormous giant many hundreds of feet high— dwarfing the trees as human beings dwarf blades of grass —strides across the horizon with one huge fist doubled, as though to crush out those who have been too stupid or too unlucky to escape his advance. He is as dreadful as the Four Horsemen of the Apocalypse.

In a less well known picture, a modern artist has de- picted a giant self-tormented. Salvador Dali's "Premoni- tion of Civil War," painted about 1936, depicts a ghastly conflict which would be unbelievable if it were not painted so superrealistically. A human body gigantic in size, towering far into the sky, has become no longer a single organism, but a pair of massive fragments like things thrown out in the dissecting room. They grip each other in a death grapple. One is only an elongated torso surmounted by a huge shock-haired head, eyes closed tight in effort and suffering, throat sinews as taut as wires: it has only one limb, a shrunken leg ending in a skeleton foot. This foot is planted firmly on the amor- phous top of a monster which has no head, but two enormous arms and hands. One of these hands is clamped around a protuberance on the dominating torso. The two half-beings are parts of a single giant, but they have split apart and are now engaged in killing, or at least in immobilizing and tormenting, each other. Fragments of the monster lie on the ground as though already torn off in the struggle. This self-murdering giant symbolizes the Spanish civil war much better than Picasso's "Guernica," which indeed displays the agony of the victims of irresistible power, but not the anguish of a nation divided against itself.

The utmost horror in Dante's hell is his confrontation with the spirit of supreme evil, Lucifer, monarch of the damned, immovable forever in the central core of the earth: a dark and loathsome giant.

H.G. Wells believed for a time that giants would surely be good. He began as a son of the age that created modern technology. Most of the time he was certain that humanity was progressing, faster and faster; and that its progress was to be measured mainly in terms of scientific development. Yet, because he was a far-sighted and highly imaginative writer, he sometimes had his doubts.* In two or three short stories written before the Wright brothers made their invention a success, he told of the drama attending the early experiments with heavier-than-air flight, and usually implied that they were bound to lead to a better life for humanity. But in *The War of the Worlds* (1898) he produced a terrifying picture of this earth invaded and temporarily dominated by superbly intelligent invaders from Mars, using not

---

*There is a good study of Wells's peculiar blend of optimism and pessimism, called *The Future as Nightmare: H. G. Wells and the Anti-Utopians*, by M. R. Hillegas (New York, 1967).

only poison gas and a heat ray, but a huge airship. ("As it flew, it rained down darkness upon the land.") Only five years after the triumph of the Wrights he wrote *The War in the Air* (1908), forecasting a worldwide conflict, in which our side (using what we now think of as regular airplanes) was beaten by the Germans using dirigible balloons of the Zeppelin type, and the Japanese employing (this is impossible, but clever of Wells) little individual wing-flapping aircraft, whose pilots, like samurai, used slashing swords. The novel ends with a picture of enormous devastation, centering on the figure of a gloomy old Englishman who has just managed to survive the fighting and the pestilence that followed, and now lives like a peasant of the darkest of the Dark Ages. He still remembers the comforts and luxuries of the vanished days of peace, which are incredible and even incomprehensible to his small grandson; and he reflects: "It didn't ought ever to 'ave begun. . . ."

Then later, Wells renewed his trust in technology, after he had watched European politics being more and more dominated by what he believed to be the irrational forces of nationalism and communism. In *The Shape of Things to Come* (1933) he pictured our world as nearly wrecked by international warfare—and then resuscitated, with the entire planet brought back to a highly satisfactory level of peace and cooperation and the fructifying exchange of goods and services. By whom? By the airmen of the world, who were determined to keep the air routes open and the planes flying, rather than see the whole worldwide network of aerial communications lapse into nullity, like the Roman aqueducts and sewers and bridges and harbor works after the collapse of the Roman empire. In Wells's vision, the airmen of the world formed themselves almost spontaneously into a supranational government.* It was a noble dream, although nowadays it seems fantastically improbable.

However, only a few years later Wells saw the destructive (and, by his standards, irrational) power of aircraft in Abyssinia and Spain; then in his own country he found air-raid shelters being dug and gas masks being issued; and finally he witnessed the brutal destruction inflicted by airmen on London and heard of the even worse destruction visited upon other cities from Rotterdam to Tokyo. Thousand-bomber raids; fire-storms lasting for hours; day-and-night bombardment; delayed-action explosives to kill people long after they had heard the All Clear. In his sad old age, he realized that the increase of man's power had not made man more intelligent, except in the matter of devising ingenious, competitive devices for inflicting pain and death, and had certainly not made man more moral. Like many simple people, he came to wish that the airplane had never been invented. After writing a profoundly pessimistic book, *Mind at the End of Its Tether,* he died sunk in an abyss of unplumbable despair. Power, he had in his youth believed, must be good. At last he perceived that power was intensely desirable, that individuals and nations and so-

---

*I do not know whether Wells was aware that Kipling had had the same idea a generation before him. See Kipling's stories "With the Night Mail: a Story of 2000 A.D." (first published in *McClure's Magazine* in 1905, then in *Actions and Reactions,* 1909) and "As Easy As A.B.C." (published in 1912, then in *A Diversity of Creatures,* 1923). "The A.B.C." (i.e., the Aerial Board of Control), "the semi-elected, semi-nominated body of a few score persons, controls the Planet. Transportation is Civilization, our motto runs." The second story, set in A.D. 2065, contains a terrifying account of the A.B.C. intimidating a rebellious part of its subject population, of course for the best motives.

cial classes would commit any infamy in order to acquire and hold it, but that it was often used for evil purposes: more and more often as it became specifically the property of a few men and a few groups, who were (he now saw) impelled by an inner drive to use it in order to dominate the rest of humanity.

In this dilemma most of mankind is caught. Most civilized people would say that we lived in an age of Progress. It is a fine ideal, progress. Like the word "evolution," it is assumed to mean "improvement." An ambitious newspaper is called *The Progressive;* institutions have celebrations to mark "a century of progress"; and any political party calling itself "progressive" will beat any party calling itself "conservative." And yet thoughtful men and women are finding it more and more difficult to define the nature of this progress which they are supposed to be enjoying.

Everyone would agree that improvements in medicine and surgery are progress. Almost everyone. Not those who suffered from the fiendish though imaginative medical experiments carried out by German physicians in concentration camps; nor anyone who has had a friend fall victim to the abuse of drugs—some of them, such as LSD, newly invented.

Many people believe that progress also means improvements in technology, such as the marvelous agricultural achievements of the United States and the machines which furnish us with so many conveniences. Scarcely a day passes that I do not bless the inventors of the typewriter, the camera, and the electric light. (When I went to school I had to write all my work laboriously and untidily in ink, and at home I studied by feeble yellow gaslight.) And yet much technology costs so much by depleting our natural resources and ravaging our natural surroundings that many sensitive people have now started to reject it as far as possible; or to limit their use of its products.

How about education? Yes, there has surely been progress in education during the last century or so. Literacy is spreading, and in most countries is continuing to spread—although some of us are already noticing that the invasion of the home by television is curtailing the amount of time and energy which the young spend on books. In most of the developed countries nowadays, one does not see that most pathetic of all sights (most pathetic, outside physical mutilation and deformity), the intelligent man or woman who would like to be able to read and write, but who is forever kept out of the world of literacy by poverty and ignorance and early neglect. In education, there is not enough progress; but there has been much. Honor to those who foresaw its advantages and its powers. Honor to those who are now carrying it on.

Medicine; technology, within limits; education and literacy; in these realms there has been progress. In what else? In social life, has there been much progress in the last fifty years? in the last hundred? (Remember, we are not talking of the United States alone but of the whole world.) In religion, have men grown better, and come closer to God? In art, are finer paintings and better buildings and nobler music being produced? Have we become better, or even wiser, in politics national and international? In morality, are we as virtuous as our ancestors were in 1900? in 1800?

It is very difficult to answer Yes. Many would say that

the world has actually grown worse in these last few generations. Take an easy example: one of the worst relationships which can exist between human beings: slavery. It has existed for thousands of years. Toward the end of the Roman empire it grew milder; and then it reappeared in another form as serfdom, an institution which dominated the Dark Ages and much of the Middle Ages. But since the Middle Ages, surely things have improved? Not so. The Russian peasants were only converted into serfs about 1600, and in the United States slavery as a trade began only twelve short generations ago. After the unremitting efforts of many great men and the short-sighted mean resistance of many small men, serfdom was abolished in Russia in 1861, and slavery in the United States about the same time. Surely that is progress? Yes; but most Russians are now serfs of the state. The ordinary citizen may not even move from one town to another without official permission. Workmen cannot strike, and dare not organize into independent unions, on the penalty of being sent to what is called a "corrective labor camp" and is in fact a colony of slaves. Solzhenitsyn has documented this system in overpowering detail, in his books on the "Gulag Archipelago." When, under Hitler, the Germans dominated much of Europe, they instituted extensive slave factories to supply their war machine: had they been victorious in 1945, they would still be running them.

One further example. When I was a schoolboy I thought that torture was a thing out of distant history and remote geography. It had been practiced far away, by savages such as the Amerindians, a revolting oddity like cannibalism; and it had been a custom among some white nations in the far past. In 1932 I went to see the medieval torture room of the Imperial Castle in Nuremberg, and gazed with horrified amazement at the racks and the pincers, and at the Iron Maiden, a hollow statue lined internally with sharp spikes so that a prisoner enclosed within her could be stabbed to death in many painful spots, as slowly as his tormentors chose. There was also an iron chair which could be heated red hot while the victim, chained and fettered, sat on it. These things are gone now, destroyed in an air raid. But in 1945 I returned to Nuremberg, and attended the trial of some men who had authorized and even administered tortures more ingenious and more devilish than these. Recently a high officer in the French army admitted using torture as a regular tactical weapon in gathering intelligence from prisoners during the Algerian war. Torture has now been reintroduced into many states which pretend to be civilized, and is practiced by men whose fathers and grandfathers would have shuddered at the very notion.*

In their hearts most intelligent people now believe that men and women are growing, not progressively better, but steadily worse. I have lived through two great wars. The first (1914–1918) was so terrible that those who took an active part in it could scarcely (in the midst of trench warfare) believe it was real, and not a hideous nightmare from which millions of human beings would, if they made a sufficient effort, awake. The second (1939–1945) was in many ways worse. The third (19??) has not

---

*On December 15, 1973, Amnesty International, the organization dedicated to assisting political prisoners, charged that torture was being used by almost half the world's governments and was spreading rapidly (*New York Times*, 16 December 1973, giving a summary of a horrifying report).

yet started. But everyone who thinks about it knows that it will be far more horrible than the other two put together. So if you were the guardian angel of Planet Earth, could you, over the past hundred years or so, report Progress?

Some even say that the more machines and power we acquire, the worse we necessarily become; but that is too easy, and it is not really true. There are some powers—such as the power to preserve life and the power to produce food—which it is very hard to misuse: although we may expect some surprises from the future experts in biological and bacteriological warfare. The truth rather is that, as we become more powerful, our lives become far more confused and far more difficult. A young man could go wrong in New York City in 1875 just as he can in 1975; but in 1875 he could not go wrong by misusing a drug which was manufactured in Marseilles according to a highly sophisticated process, imported by smugglers using jet planes, and distributed by superefficient sales methods.

This gloomy spectacle suggests one lesson which we ought to teach the young, and to bear constantly in mind ourselves. This is the lesson that moral and spiritual progress is infinitely more difficult than technological progress; and that, even surrounded and served by intricate and marvelous machines, man may be little more than a cruel and clever ape—unless he constantly thinks about what is truly good and strives to attain it.

That is the lesson which the great books, above almost all other possessions of the human spirit, are designed to teach. It is not possible to study them—beginning with Homer and the Bible and coming down to the magnificent novels of yesterday *(War and Peace)* and of today *(Doctor Faustus)*—without realizing, first, the existence of permanent moral and intellectual standards; second, the difficulty of maintaining them in one's own life; and, third, the necessity of preserving them against their chief enemies, folly and barbarism.

Barbarism we know. It is widespread over large parts of the globe; it always has been; it is a constant threat: we strike it down in Germany, it reappears in the Middle East. But folly and stupidity are harder to recognize as dangers, because they are all round us, besieging us every moment of our lives. One reason why our profession as teachers is so exhausting is that we are constantly working against the tide, trying to make people think. Thinking is a pleasure, and an ingredient of the highest happiness; but it is an uncommon pleasure, and a difficult one to appreciate. In most countries it has two chief enemies: the competition of simpler pleasures, and the prevalence of wrongheaded theories of education. Of the simpler pleasures there is no need to speak at length. But there is one particular danger in educational theory, against which our reverence for the great books must be defended. This is the notion of education by doing instead of thinking. In practice this often means that teachers are happy when their pupils are engaged in more or less harmless social activity, and that they do not want them to sit alone, reading and learning to think, through assimilating other men's and women's thoughts and then forming their own ideas. Many professional educators write such ghastly English that it is evident they have never read a decent book in their lives.* Some of them would positively repudiate the concept that any real wisdom could be gained from reading a book written several hundred or even several thousand years ago; and, still more vehemently, the notion that it is the duty of teachers to keep the flow of such wisdom moving steadily and constantly through the minds of generation after generation of pupils. They would not believe that that was progress. Such people are working toward an era in which the feeling of intellectual responsibility will be destroyed; but they are wrong, and they will be proven wrong. Just as it is our duty to be healthy, it is our duty to be wise.

°

*See J. D. Koerner, *The Miseducation of American Teachers* (Boston, 1963), especially "L'Envoi: English or Educanto?"

THE
LIBERAL
TEACHER

What should be the character of the ideal teacher? What kind of man or woman is best fitted to give a liberal education?

This is a serious question, both for teachers and for the general public. Teachers are respected; not always admired. We are praised for regularity and a sense of duty; but most people do not necessarily expect us to be bright. Doctors are held in honor, and lawyers are esteemed for their sharp intelligence; but teachers are sometimes thought of as respectable drudges—like hospital nurses, or even like attendants in an asylum for the harmless insane. Yet they have high ideals, and often suffer in pursuing them. The man in the street scarcely realizes that many forms of business, some major industries, and one or two minor professions could be completely abolished without gravely injuring American society; whereas the disappearance—or even what we see in some quarters, the continuous neglect and degradation

—of the teaching profession must mean a disaster to the entire nation. If the average man can be made to understand that our careers, although ill rewarded, are not merely unsuccessful attempts to make money, but are endeavors to attain a difficult set of ideals, ideals valuable to the whole community, perhaps he will take us, and his responsibilities to us, more seriously than he and his elected representatives now do.

The question is serious, and well worth the effort involved in trying to find an answer to it. Yet it cannot be answered precisely. There is not even a single answer to it. The definition of the liberal educator is, and ought to be, different in different countries of the world. His or her task in India would be disparate from his task in Sweden, and that again from his task in Brazil. And it is highly possible that the ideal teacher would be different in different parts of the United States—in so far as our country is not, and is not trying to become, a single monolithic unity, but a federation of individual regions which allow for variations of custom and character. Different, the answers to the question may be; but we shall not expect to find them conflicting with one another. A good doctor in Calcutta is unlike a good doctor in Detroit; but ultimately the two have the same purpose in life. In the same way, even if the answers to this question are different in various countries, and even in various sections of the United States, we shall expect to find them convergent, rather than inharmonious or contrary. Basically, all liberal educators are trying to do the same thing.

We are searching, not for the ideal teacher of *any* subject under the sun (boxing, hydrostatics, nursing, logic), but for the ideal teacher of the liberal subjects: the teacher who is best capable of giving a liberal education.

This is the type of education which does not necessarily fit a man or woman to earn money, but prepares them to do what is ultimately more important and more difficult—to live well, using *all* their capacities. Aristotle points out that the art (or skill, or technique) of making money is different from other arts or skills or techniques, such as medicine; it is wrong to assume that a man or woman who practices one art (such as medicine) must be expert, or even want to be expert, in the art of making money.* This distinction, oversimplified though it may be, illuminates the difference between liberal and technical education. There are all kinds of skills which can be taught, and which will help the men and women who acquire them to make a living; but if these men and women have not also a liberal education, they are little better than clever slaves. The word "liberal" means "fitted for a free man," one who is not a slave to a machine or to an office or to a single money-making skill.

It would be a mistake to set the teacher's ideal uncomfortably high: for it is terribly discouraging (and in our profession there are many discouragements, to which it would be injurious to add) to learn that the ideal teacher would be endowed with so many admirable qualities that no human being could possibly realize them all. We are looking for the optimum character and accomplishment which, with proper application and decent luck, could be attained by a teacher who saw it clearly in his mind. Therefore we begin with the essentials.

There are some qualities which every teacher ought to possess—or to train himself to possess. These are the

---

*Politics 1256.

qualities which he wants his pupils to acquire.

The young learn much (more than they realize) by the silent power of example. In all professions this is understood. A surgeon does not explain to his students that it is their duty to be deft and neat and economical of action. When he does an operation, he is deft and neat: he economizes on effort, and on motion, and on pain. By watching him, the learners realize that they must imitate him until they too possess these qualities. In the U.S. Marine Corps training course for officers, one of the most powerful lessons is never spoken aloud. It is instilled simply by the force of example. By watching senior officers, the young officer candidates learn that they are expected to become taut and keen and energetic; and yet easy in their manner. The Romans, too, in higher education, leaned strongly upon the instinct of mimicry. A youth who hoped to become a statesman was not given a mass of books to read, or a ton of theory to assimilate. He was expected to spend his days respectfully and silently observing a mature man, a distinguished public servant, to whom he was something between a secretary and an adopted son, and on whose character he could gradually mold his own.

Obviously, therefore, a teacher must have regular habits: regular without being machinelike. Young people tend to be sloppy and even anarchical. They feel that all order is imposed upon them from outside and is crushing out their natural love of life. In a state of anomia* they

---

*The word is Greek and simply means "lawlessness"—worse than anarchy, which means a society in which there is no ruler but (the anarchists hope) natural order prevails. It appears in our dictionaries as anomie, doubtless because it came into our language from French or German, which transform the Greek final -a into a final -e. Ogden

may be happy for a time; but they will never fulfill their best capacities. If their teachers are obviously living regularly and effectively and happily, the pupils will learn (then or later) to live in the same way. Many a boy whose home life was a morass of untidiness and improvisation, because his parents were not house trained, has escaped from it and shaped his own character and career satisfactorily, because he admired and imitated a teacher whose life was orderly and yet humane and satisfying.

The teacher ought also to believe in the power of the human will. The young are creatures of impulse. It is fatiguing for them to execute one single feat of will power (more fatiguing in the moral and intellectual realm than in the field of physical exercise);* it is even more fatiguing for them to cultivate the steady execution of consistently willed plans. Nearly all of them lack confidence in their own will power. Some of them scarcely understand how much can be achieved by the will, even if it is imperfectly trained. Many of them shrink from the effort involved in consistent living, recoil from it all through their careers, and drift from youth to middle age to death like a ship which is all sails and mast, without a rudder. Yet, if the teacher is a man or woman of strong will power, he/she will show them

---

Nash summed it up in a witty couplet: "In the world of mules, there are no rules." We could say "anomy" on the model of "economy" and "autonomy," but the word is hard to pronounce and is too easily confused with "enemy" and even "enema."

*In my memory bank I still have a picture (was it a cartoon, or a real visual experience?) of a big lummox sitting in his room in college, glaring at a manual of economics which he held in his left hand, while grasping a football (his darling and the center of his life purpose) in his right.

what can be achieved, even in adversity, by determination. Both by example and by precept it is the duty of the liberal teacher to instill in his pupils a conviction of the value and power of the controlled human will. The connection between will power and teaching, the connection between will power and intellectual work generally, has not always been recognized. In the present time, because of our dangerous slide into complete permissiveness both in the home and in the school, it tends to be ignored or denied; yet the best teachers have always been aware of it. It was a famous American teacher, Ralph Waldo Emerson, who said:

> That book is good
> Which puts me in a working mood.
> Unless to Thought is added Will,
> Apollo is an imbecile.*

A liberal education is based largely on training the mind. Therefore the good teacher will let it be clearly seen that he believes in the power of the mind and the satisfactions of spiritual life. He will be an intellectual. He will enjoy books, and he will go on enlarging and refining his taste throughout his life. I remember that it was a revelation to me in my middle teens when I discovered, simply from observing the behavior of one of my teachers in the school library, that there existed what W.B. Yeats called "the fascination of what's difficult." Certain books, certain types of thought and emotion expressed in words, were (I realized) intended to be obscure; meant to be grappled with; would always present

---

The Poet.

problems; and yet, in their very complexities and in-
solubilities, contained delight. A good teacher will be a
man who is happy when he is alone in a library.

Furthermore, a humane educator will delight in the
fine arts, and will either practice religion or respect religion. He will not deliberately refrain from uttering the
word "beauty" or the word "God." He need not be constantly proclaiming them, nor need he emphasize them
and expound them at great length. With high matters,
restraint of speech is good. The ideal scholar whom
Chaucer described was not a gasbag:

Noght o word spak he more than was nede,
And that was seyd in forme and reverence,
And short and quik, and ful of hy sentence.*

Even without long speeches, the young can very soon
detect when one of their teachers is a man or woman
who secretly despises art and history and literature and
the life of the mind, and who thinks religion is at best a
matter of formal observance. Though it is possible that
they may merely scorn him or her for this, it is also a
grave danger that they may come to imitate their
teacher, and so deny themselves many of the highest
satisfactions and exaltations of this life.

Many theorists have written about education as if it
were chiefly intended to teach young people to live in
society. Of course that is one of its purposes. Social living
is complex and difficult. Yet it is clear, when we look at
young men and women, that they also need to be taught
how to live with themselves. Many of the most impor-

---

*"The Clerk of Oxenford," *Prologue to the Canterbury Tales,* 304–306.

tant things in life happen to us in solitude. Intellectual discoveries, powerful emotional experiences, enlargements of the soul, come more commonly to a man or a woman alone in a quiet room or sitting in the heart of wild nature, than in the restless and noisy and often thoughtless group. (Is this one of the weaknesses of Protestantism as compared with Roman Catholicism, that it provides very little for those who need to be alone?) When it arrives, the good society will ensure every one of us both life in common, and the equally precious life of privacy. The teacher who wishes to open and expand the hearts of his pupils ought himself to show that he respects and enjoys both these complementary styles of life.

All these, and others too, are the moral and intellectual qualities which the good teacher will possess. The young teacher has few of them, if any. Yet, if he or she knows that it is his duty to acquire them and to learn how to practice them—in just the same way as he learns the niceties of his own special subject—he or she will do so; and, when he is mature, will exercise them with the same confidence an experienced surgeon enjoys when he operates, with something of the same devotion as that which fills the heart of a minister when he offers up a prayer.

Turn now to harder and more complex questions. Is it possible to define the attitude of the ideal teacher to society? to his subject? to his pupils?

We have been told, and some of us have believed, that in his attitude to society the teacher should be militant: that he ought to be a strong advocate of immediate change, the architect of a new world, and, in fact, something close to an active revolutionary. This view was common, and indeed compulsory, in Germany during the National Socialist regime; it is now mandatory in Russia and her satellite states, and it is being (against some resistance) introduced into China, too. Without looking very far, we can trace it in some of the books about the theory of education which appeared both in the United States and in Europe during the 1930s and 1940s; and in the behavior of some of the younger teachers during the student disorders of the 1960s.

Is this principle justified by the careers of distinguished teachers of the past? Have they been politically active inside their classrooms? Have they been revolutionaries?

Usually they have not. Men and women who felt strongly that a radical political change was needed have usually detached themselves from education altogether, and have adopted the more direct methods of electioneering and propagandizing among adult citizens. Some teachers have been convinced conservatives in politics. Some have stood utterly outside the distracting world of political change. Some have been, during their spare time, active in political organizations, but have said little or nothing of their work to their classes. Most good teachers have apparently felt that education and politics do not mix, at least in school, and have been reticent about current political issues.

On the other hand many distinguished teachers have been devoted to the cause of social reform, to the abolition of unearned and unjustified privilege, to the fuller utilization of all the human resources of their countries. Even when they were convinced that it was desirable to maintain the political structure of their times, they were often eager to make it more flexible, to induce it to nurture and to employ talents which might otherwise be wasted. For instance, the great Jesuit teachers of the seventeenth century were, or appeared to be, in favor of maintaining monarchy and aristocracy, whether in Spain or in China, but they wished to make both monarchs and noblemen into good and intelligent men, and to see them supported and assisted by the brains of other good and intelligent men, however humble their origins. It is in the field of social reform rather than politics that a teacher, if his interests lie in that direction, can be most effective. Take a simple but striking instance. Which has produced the more remarkable effects on our civilization: the political agitation that led to the establishment of votes for women, or the slower and less spectacular social and educational movement that caused the admission of women into every institution of higher education?

It is well to make this point clear, because the word "liberal" has frequently been misused by political writers. It has even been suggested that a liberal education ought to be controlled by the principles of those political parties which preempt the word "liberal" in their titles or their programs. This is a mistake, and it is a dangerous mistake. The true liberal respects the maximum development of every human being. Necessarily, therefore, he is opposed to the regulation of every citizen's life by an all-embracing system of law and to the control of all his activities by the all-seeing (though not all-wise) state. The worship of government is not liberalism, and is in fact opposed to those principles which are truly liberal.

Can we define the attitude of the ideal teacher to his subject? Surely we can. It seems clear that the liberal educator will have two beliefs, and demonstrate them constantly in word and act.

The first is the firm conviction that the subject he or she teaches is genuinely and permanently important. The teacher of French who never reads a French book for pleasure, the teacher of history who does not enjoy visiting historic sites and examining original documents, are frauds; and their pupils soon detect their fraudulence. Imagine if, when you consulted your doctor about symptoms of illness which you had detected in yourself, you saw quite clearly from his perfunctory manner and his vague conversation that he not only did not care in the slightest whether you suffered pain or not, but thought the whole health business was simply a routine which he went through in order to get money and prestige. You would leave him at once, and you would have a lowered opinion of the medical profession. Yet there are many teachers like that doctor: men and women who have no interest in their own subject and no respect for it. They teach it because it provides a salary and prepares for a pension; otherwise it bores and even disgusts them. Such an attitude also bores and disgusts their pupils—with the additional danger that the pupils may well come to be bored and disgusted with all education and with all intellectual activity. By a five-minute inspection of a teacher's bookshelves, you and I can tell whether he has any interest in his subject or not. The young can tell after listening to him for a few hours: sometimes even for a few minutes. No, the good teacher believes in his subject and is genuinely, unashamedly enthusiastic about it. He will not shrink from saying to his pupils:

> I give you the end of a golden string;
>   Only wind it into a ball—
> It will lead you into Heaven's gate,
>   Built in Jerusalem's wall.*

Here we must make a distinction which is not always recognized, but is vitally important. The subjects of a liberal education are valuable for two different reasons and ought to be taught for two different reasons.

One is that they are precious parts of our culture. They must be kept alive in our minds, for their own sake. It would be a miserable country which neglected history so as to forget the meaning of its own past; or neglected languages so as to be unable to read the writings of other nations and to enter into their thoughts.

But it is also important for the teacher to train other teachers—scholars and communicators who will continue to explore and to explain the subject to which he has devoted himself.

In colleges and universities here and in Europe one sometimes sees that these two different principles are confused. There are some teachers who regard their own subject as though it could not possibly improve the mind of the average young man and woman or contain any intellectual interest for the public in general. Their sole interest, besides doing research, is to produce other researchers. This is mistaken. And it is equally mistaken to talk of a subject as though it were of broad general interest, but could not capture the attention of any student enough to make him devote his life to working in it. Once again, the parallel with medicine is instructive.

---

*Blake, *Jerusalem* 4, preface.

The best teachers of medicine want to produce both the general practitioners who will apply the principles of their art to relieving pain and preserving life, and the discoverers who will make further explorations in the field and pass increased knowledge on to the next generation. So the liberal educator will aim at maintaining the importance of his subject (whatever it may be) both by making it known to all his pupils as part of their cultural equipment, and by stimulating a few of them to make it their life's work.

The second conviction which ought to fill the mind of the ideal teacher, with reference to his subject, is that it is broad rather than narrow, deep rather than shallow, infinite rather than limited. Only those who teach very young children should try to convince their pupils that everything can be found out and understood. Those who teach young men and women should let it be seen that they believe complete knowledge is desirable but unattainable.

Some fine teachers have held that their subjects could conceivably be known in their entirety. St. Thomas Aquinas held that, although both God and matter were mysteries, the universe between them could be wholly understood and explained; and many Jewish teachers have considered that all important knowledge, all, was contained in the Hebrew scriptures and the Talmud. Yet they and others who thought in the same way have always added that the human mind is imperfect. Outside the great mysteries, all can be known; but where is the mind that can know it? St. Thomas himself toward the end of his life abandoned research and writing, because he had a revelation which showed him how inadequate even his own powerful intellect really was.

Nowadays, however, we take the other point of view. The knowable, we believe, is inexhaustible. No subject can ever be completely understood, and the reason must be kept flexible by constantly grappling with an eternally novel reality. The most original of recent philosophical teachers, Henri Bergson, has put this in a curious image:

> Reality is growth, total and indivisible; progressive invention; duration: comparable with an elastic balloon gradually expanding and at each moment assuming an unexpected form.*

One of the essentials of learning is the constant perception of novelty: so that the whole process of education might well be adapted to the picture of the physical universe which is suggested in Bergson's image and described by certain modern astronomers: an assemblage of constantly changing factors and forces, never static, ceaselessly interacting, and expanding toward infinity.

Accordingly the liberal educator will both encourage and discipline his pupils by explaining to them that their minds deserve every respect, and yet can attain only an approximation to the truth; that the world, or even their one particular subject, is greater than any single brain can ever grasp. This is one of the best lessons that any teacher can give his pupils: particularly nowadays, when so much imperfect knowledge and inadequately sifted data and prejudiced guesswork masquerade under the name of "science." So much harm has been done in the

---

*From *Le Possible et le réel*, *Oeuvres*, Pléïade edition (Paris, 1963), p. 1335.

world by those who believed that they were in posses-
sion of the whole truth, and that those who differed from
them were absolutely and wickedly wrong. We should
always remember what Oliver Cromwell wrote to that
august body, the General Assembly of the Church of
Scotland:

> I beseech you, in the bowels of Christ, think it possi-
> ble you may be mistaken.

Yes, and even more. The effective teacher of the humane
subjects may acknowledge the imperfection of knowledge by confessing his own errors and oversights. He
may even admit his own prejudices—no, not prejudices,
but considered preferences. The teacher of algebra can
scarcely show a preference for one type of equation over
another; but the historian and other teachers of liberal
subjects can with advantage make it clear that they believe one period more fertile, one creative artist more
admirable than another. They should not expect their
students to follow their choices blindly, but rather hope
to stimulate them into criticism and creative disagree-
ment.

In his attitude to his subject, then, the ideal teacher
will be a liberal traditionalist. He will explain to the
students (and to himself) that the subject he teaches is
important; that its central truths are reasonably well
established; that it is in its totality beyond the range of
human comprehension; but that it may interest some of
them enough to become their life's work, and must improve and uplift all of them by becoming part of their
spiritual capital.

The third problem in the work of the liberal educator is his attitude to his pupils. And this can best be defined by examining what the best teachers of the past have done: what they have felt about their pupils, and how they have treated them.

Almost universally we find that they have not had a single relationship to their pupils, but rather a double one. They have maintained a tension composed of complementary feelings; and the difficulty of being a good teacher is largely due to the fact that it is hard to maintain such a tension without suffering oneself or making the pupils suffer.

For instance, the best teachers give their pupils both a sense of order, discipline, control; and a powerful stimulus which urges them to take their destinies in their own hands, kick over all rules, and transgress all boundaries. Sometimes their pupils complain that they do not know what is wanted: are they to be puppets? or original geniuses? partners? or subdued subservient apprentices? The answer is that their teachers want to accustom them to both the essential types of mental activity: self-surrender to an external aim and purpose, and free development of their individual talents.

Some teachers have determined (often unconsciously) to dominate and crush and enslave their pupils, while others have tried in excessive modesty to diminish themselves entirely so as to build up the ego of their students. In Ved Mehta's *Fly and the Fly-Bottle* (Boston, 1963) there is a striking study of the late Polish-Jewish-English historian Lewis Namier. Much of the reminiscent information about him is provided by John Brooke, a devoted collaborator who is carrying on his work. Mehta records that, although Namier has been dead for years, Brooke is unable to realize it, and constantly says: "Sir Lewis works very hard. . . . Sir Lewis believes. . . ." Both this extreme and the other are mistaken. Good teachers challenge their pupils as rivals, and thus combine the best of the two attitudes. They hope that they themselves will be equaled and even transcended. One of the finest rewards of the teacher is to see his pupils excelling himself.

Another tension in teaching is that between the group and the individual. However much the teacher is tempted to treat the exceptional pupil (whether very good or very bad) as a special case and to devote to him or her a great deal of time and attention, he must remember that this is not his sole duty, and usually is not his main duty. His first obligation is to his class: to the group. Within the class, he should learn to bring out the personalities and answer the special needs of each of the young people who are his pupils: he must make them feel that they are understood as individuals. But at the same time he must make them realize that they are part of a larger organization, and in some ways subordinate to it.

In our work there are many more of these tensions. Most of the mistakes committed in teaching are made by those who believe that no such tensions exist or ought to exist. But the relation between teacher and pupil is a human relationship, and no relationship between human beings is ever simple.

In fact, there is a tension between antitheses in the entire process of education. Education means a recognition of the force and value of traditional knowledge; but it also means a will to create and to advance what is new. The liberal educator knows that there is a central core of transmitted knowledge and discernment, without which his pupils can scarcely exist as human beings; but he also knows that this body of transmitted beliefs must always be subject to criticism and revision, and will always profit from addition. Such development continues permanently through the existence of the human race.

Still we have not mentioned nearly all the qualities which the liberal educator ought to have. We might suggest that he should be trained to eat grass and to grow a thick coat of fur: so that he could live on his meager salary, without wasting it on buying expensive food and clothing; or that he should have no wife and family but spend each summer as a rootless hitch-hiker, thereby becoming able (without going bankrupt) to visit the big libraries and the foreign lands which provide so much of his spiritual nourishment. (There are teachers of French and Spanish, Latin and Greek, who have worked for many years without ever seeing the countries whose spirits they have been endeavoring to evoke.) From the Bible we learn that "to obey is better than sacrifice, and to hearken than the fat of rams."* This is good authority for the value of teaching to the pupils; but teachers are not rewarded with the fat of rams, or anything like the value of the time and effort which they expend.

Seriously, however, the most important qualification of the liberal educator is neither helped nor hindered by his poverty: perhaps it is even encouraged by his being hard up. This is that he must be an individual. He must not be a machine. He must not be a rubber stamp. He must not repeat the thoughts of others. He must not even repeat his own thoughts. Life is change within permanence, and the individual therefore must change within

*1 Samuel 15:22.

a fixed pattern of ideals. The liberal teacher is not a type, but an individual. We can see how true this is by looking back over a long roster of distinguished teachers. We are bound to remember with gratitude and admiration such men as George Kittredge of Harvard, who made Shakespeare's plays familiar to forty generations of students, and thereby helped to raise the standards of dramatic and literary appreciation throughout the United States; and George Pierce Baker of Yale, who taught so many American dramatists to write admirable plays—or at least to write. (One of these two men was essentially a transmitter and interpreter of traditional values, the other a creator of new powers; yet the former was boldly original, while the latter was convinced of the values of tradition.) Some of the effective teachers are anonymous, or nearly so. Such was Thomas Jenkins, the eccentric but apparently stimulating master who taught Latin to William Shakespeare, who outlined to him the noble and fantastic myths of Greece and Rome, and who gave him lofty ideals of narration and description by introducing him to Ovid and Vergil; who inspired him with that sense which creates greatness, the sense that there are always fresh worlds to conquer.

Surely it is difficult to become a good teacher. Yet it is a poorly rewarded profession. Two of the four learned vocations are meagerly rewarded and little respected, while two are admired and well paid. Doctors and lawyers are usually comfortable. Some of them become rich. Teachers and priests or ministers remain poor, and are not even expected to acquire wealth. Lawyers and doctors are engaged in preserving men's and women's lives and property; while teachers and clergymen do but help to furnish their minds and their souls. Lawyers and doctors intervene in crises, when men or women are suddenly beset by danger and will give up almost anything to be set free of it. Clergymen and teachers are not occupied in meeting crises, but rather in maintaining and perfecting what already exists. Lawyers and doctors can wreck a life by a single mistake which can be made in an hour. Teachers and clergymen make mistakes too; but these are slow-building errors, which do not mature for months, and are supposed to be easier to avoid, easier to remedy. Yet they may be just as serious in the end; and the good that teachers and clergymen do may be more lasting than anything done by physicians and lawyers.

It is shameful that we are so poorly paid, and on the whole so little respected. Nevertheless—although we ought to protest against that disability and search for means of removing it—it is the reflex of several hard facts. One of these facts is that, more than the lawyers and the doctors, teachers are selfless people, giving out of themselves far more than they ever expect to get back. It is because we know that the world partly depends on such people that we chose our profession. The other fact is that men will pay more to be delivered from danger than to be assisted in developing themselves. Men and women can see dangers, but they cannot assess their powers. It is our task to show them what they scarcely realize: their enormous potentialities, intellectual, aesthetic, spiritual; and those of their children. That is our task. To accomplish it even in part will be our best reward.

THE
SCHOLARLY
LIFE

It is a curious life we lead, the life of scholarship. Difficult and demanding, most certainly; frustrating, far too often for comfort; poorly rewarded in material terms; and calling for a great deal of spiritual stamina. Sometimes I ask myself how many of my colleagues would, if given an opportunity to change their careers and take up some quite different vocation, accept, and abandon the world of scholarship. My friend Moses Hadas and I were both tempted. We had been away from Columbia on leave in different areas during World War II; and although we both continued to read Greek and Latin whenever there was an opportunity (just as a professional musician would try to get in some practice every day), we had after some years fallen out of touch with the new books, and the current periodicals, and such research as was still going on. And of course we were both far, far removed from both libraries and classrooms. Meanwhile we had been acquiring different skills, and had found ourselves to be competent in new and unexpected fields. When we were being released from military (or paramilitary) service, each of us separately was offered two or three new jobs. They paid better salaries than we could expect as professors, and in some ways they seemed to be more important. Without consulting each other, we both thought over the proposals for some time, and then turned them down to return to Columbia. I never regretted this decision, nor as far as I know did Moses Hadas; but it was not an easy decision to make. One consideration in particular made it difficult. We both remembered how, after the *first* World War, the young soldiers returning had piled into colleges and universities, not so much to study as to have a high old time; and how hard in that rackety atmosphere it had been both to teach them and to maintain the steady pace of scholarly research. We were afraid that the soldiers of the *second* World War—which was for Americans a far more serious and long-drawn-out affair than the first— might prove, when they entered college, to be unteachable, resistant to authority, and contemptuous of intellectual work. For us to return to Columbia as professors, and to find that we had to try to teach a gang of war-weary or war-hardened veterans, who had been long removed from the world of the mind and conditioned to reject or evade discipline wherever possible, would have been a sore trial. But it turned out the exact opposite. The ex-soldiers who came in on the G.I. Bill became the keenest and most intelligent students we had ever had, or even hoped to have. Those were the days when the Humanities program in Columbia College really flourished. Moses Hadas and I both taught Humanities as well as Greek and Latin; and in those postwar years we had the experience, so rare and precious for teachers, that we got from our classes almost as much stimulus as we gave them.

In ways like these, the academic life is rewarding. But it is undoubtedly difficult. The main reason is this. It forces us to combine two different activities. These demand two sets of qualifications, which are in some ways interconnected, but in other ways quite alien to each other. Learning is one of these activities, hard enough in itself. The other is teaching, also a hard job. Few men and few women have minds large enough and characters sufficiently firm yet flexible to cope with them both at once.

Consider first the life of learning. It is based on certain principles which people outside the academic field seldom fully understand or appreciate.

The first of these is *devotion:* devotion and diligence. The Germans pithily call it *Sitzfleisch*, "flesh to sit on," because they admire the will power that keeps a man at his desk or laboratory table hour after hour, while he penetrates inch by inch to the heart of a problem. But many of us now find that *Sitzfleisch* is not so important as what newspapermen call "legwork"—the patient unremitting pursuit of a set of facts from book to book, from one library to another, sometimes even from one country to another, until they are caught and nailed down. The principle is summed up in a quaint anecdote from a bygone era. In the year 1847 President Martin Routh of Magdalen College, Oxford, had reached the age of ninety-two without losing his faculties or his position as president. (He was so old that he remembered seeing Samuel Johnson as an undergraduate.) One of his students approached him with respectful deference, saying: "Mr. President, give me leave to ask a question I have sometimes asked of aged persons, but never of any so aged or so learned as yourself. Every studious man has had occasion to experience the special value of some one axiom or precept. Would you mind giving me the benefit of such a word of advice?" Routh thought for a while. Then he replied: "I think, sir, since you care for the advice of an old man, sir, you will find it a very good practice [here he looked the student archly in the face] *always to verify your references,* sir!"*

Like most ideals, the ideal of devotion has its comic side. The classicist Ingram Bywater used to complain that some of his colleagues had "a dithguthting appetite for *facts.*" Both the nobility and the unworldliness of the devoted scholar are summed up in a poem by one of the greatest English comic poets, Robert Browning. As the specialist in Greek grammar is carried to his grave, his students, bearing the bier, sing how even while he was dying he continued his research.

> So, with the throttling hands of Death at strife,
>   Ground he at grammar;
> Still, thro' the rattle, parts of speech were rife.
>   While he could stammer,
> He settled Hoti's business—let it be!—
>   Properly based Oun,
> Gave us the doctrine of the enclitic De,
>   Dead from the waist down.†

---

*J. W. Burgon, *Lives of Twelve Good Men* (New York, 1891), p. 38. Routh lived from 1755 to 1854, just missing his century.

†Browning, "A Grammarian's Funeral." *Hoti, Oun,* and *De* are small but essential words in ancient Greek—here pronounced in the old manner, as though it were English.

Or it might be put in a livelier way. As Lord Halifax said: "the struggling for knowledge has a pleasure in it like that of wrestling with a fine woman."

It is amazing, and sometimes appalling, to lesser men when they see the exacting routine and the formidable achievements of such a devoted scholar. One of the most impressive in the classical field was Isaac Casaubon, who died in 1614 at the relatively early age of fifty-five, leaving a very moving diary of his daily work together with sixty hand-written volumes containing his notes on the Greek and Latin books he had studied.* This was not mechanical copying, but intelligent abstracting and commenting. He himself declared that it was the only sure method of checking failures of recollection, adding: "No one knows any more than he holds in his memory."† In modern science there have been many such paragons of diligence: for example, Thomas Hunt Morgan, who won the Nobel Prize for establishing the chromosome theory of heredity. Together with two student-colleagues, Bridges and Sturtevant, he reared hundreds of generations of Drosophila, the fruit fly, through an unbroken series of seventeen years, keeping them in a single room at Columbia University, giving them an annual vacation at Woods Hole, Massachusetts, and at last using one of the humblest of creatures to prove one of the most important facts about physical life on this planet.‡

———————————

*Casaubon resembles Browning's Grammarian, for he died of internal complications attributable to the fact that he often sat studying for many hours without evacuating his internal secretions.

†*Tantum quisque scit quantum memoria tenet.*

‡A.H. Sturtevant, "Thomas Hunt Morgan, 1866–1945," *National Academy of Sciences, Biographical Memoirs* 33 (1959), 283–325.

There are two different methods of arranging and shaping a career thus devoted to scholarship. Some young scholars are not clearly aware of this difference, and do not know that they must make a choice.

Suppose you write a book on a large theme, which you feel to be important: the age of Jefferson; the concept of Mind; the theory of business-cycles; West African kinship-systems. Suppose, further, that it is reasonably well received, and that the publisher tells you he will have to reprint it. Of course you will correct any misprints and false attributions and factual errors which you and your reviewers have detected. But what more should you do? Now (if not before) you must make the decision. Should you make substantial changes in the book, to meet important objections raised by critics? And thereafter should you go on concentrating on the same subject, reading and (when invited) reviewing all the new books on it which other scholars bring out, searching for fresh material and new arguments to improve your original work, updating it every three or four years so that it goes into a second, a fourth, a sixth edition—in fact, should you spend your life rewriting your book, so as to ensure that it continues to hold a secure, perhaps even a dominating, place in the field?

Or, having once covered the theme, should you follow the example of Pontius Pilate, saying: "What I have written I have written"? And should you then move on and explore a different field, which presents the charm and the challenge of novelty?

To make the choice between these two methods is partly a matter of disposition, of character. The chemist Wilhelm Ostwald divided scholarly explorers into romantics and classics, implying that the different concepts of research held by different scientists were shaped by their temperaments. Will you decide (as Swift put it) to resemble a spider, spinning out endless webs from its own vitals, or a bee, visiting flower after flower and extracting a different sweetness from each of them? Will you be like those individualists one sees out west in Colorado and Wyoming, who dig their own little vertical mine shafts into the earth, and spend the rest of their days extracting ore from the same small vein? Or will you be a wandering prospector, trying first this mountain range and then that, never working out a single lode but always adventuring farther forward?

The answer lies partly in your character; but also in your conception of strategy. It depends what kind of impact you wish to make upon your own area of scholarship. For young scholars faced with such a choice, there is one device which may help them to decide. This is to study the careers of eminent men among their predecessors, and select one or two models to emulate. If they are Greek and Latin scholars, they may determine to follow the example of Housman, who spent most of his professional career in producing incisive and penetrating texts of three and only three Latin poets (whom, incidentally, he did not much admire); or they may rather choose to follow Norden and Wilamowitz, who produced a steady flow of ambitious books and interpretative articles, very rarely turned back to revise and reedit any of their publications, and constantly surprised even their admirers by the novelty of their work and the fertility of their intellect.

It is good for us to study the lives of elder scholars. As well as giving us hints on career strategy, it helps to teach us the second principle of scholarship, which is *humility.*

The founder of scientific medicine, Hippocrates, stated the ground of this principle in the famous aphorism: "The life so short, the craft so long to learn."* Never shall I forget a conference held by the New York Academy of Medicine, where I was privileged to hear some specialists discussing their Hippocratic craft. A friend presented me to the senior physician of the group, who was about seventy-five years old, and told me that he was an expert on the structure and functions of the human brain. The old man smiled, and said: "If I live to be a hundred and retain my faculties, I think I might begin to understand something about the central nervous system."

Indeed, the problems which we study would be difficult enough even if they remained static; but they grow, and change, and interact, so that only a very immature or conceited scholar can now think of "mastering the subject." We should all do well to remember the snub administered by that fine Platonist William Hepworth Thompson to the arrogant young philosopher G.W. Balfour: "We are none of us infallible—not even the youngest of us."

The third principle of scholarship is far easier to apply now than it has ever been throughout history. This is *organization.*

The pattern of intellectual systematization was first set in the western world by Aristotle. Before him there

---

*Hippocrates, *Aphorisms* i.i; Chaucer's rendering, *Parlement of Foules* i.

had been small groups of specialists like the Hippocratic school of physicians; Plato and others had formed societies of intellectuals with shared interests; but it was Aristotle who first envisaged the world of knowledge as a whole composed of separate areas, each of which could be intensively studied; who realized that, before any one of these could be investigated, brute facts must be assembled; and who set his colleagues and students to assemble them. Most of us, in so far as we are scholars, are Aristotelians. Plato the poet wrote a book about an ideal state with a perfect constitution, created by his mind and the mind of his teacher, Socrates—a state which, he acknowledged, would never come into existence unless by an almost Messianic miracle.* Aristotle, the physician's son, assisted by pupils and colleagues, collected the actual constitutions of 158 real states; in his book *Politics* he drew conclusions from this factual material.†

In establishing systematic research, one important further step was taken by the Greek scholars who worked in the Museum (= the Shrine of the Muses) in the new city of Alexandria. It was they who created the first great library in the Mediterranean world, sought for authentic manuscripts, collected texts, copied archives, and compiled hundreds of reference books. And they did not confine themselves to literature and history. Endowed by the Macedonian kings of Egypt, the Museum was the first university in our world, housing experts in

---

*Plato, *Rep.* 7. 540d–541b5; 9. 592a8–592b6.

†Aristotle's *Politics* is not so much a book as a collection of treatises: some are speculations about the ideal state, but others (Books 4–6) are based on empirical study of existing constitutions. See E. Barker, *The Politics of Aristotle* (Oxford, 1946), Appendix V. iii, and W. Jaeger, *Aristotle* (tr. R. Robinson, Oxford, 1948²), cc. 10 and 13.

mathematics and astronomy (Conon of Samos) and poly-maths such as Eratosthenes, who calculated the circumference of the earth, set up the first systematic chronological scheme of history, and investigated the prime numbers.*

It is really only in the last century and a half that modern scholarship has overtaken and passed the intellectual organization of those Alexandrian scholars. The chief modern representative of this ideal in the humanistic field was that imperial figure, the historian Christian Mathias Theodor Mommsen, who died in 1903 after a long and marvelous life of nearly ninety years, during which he accomplished as much as ten ordinary savants.† His masterpiece of organization was to send teams of researchers all over the Western world to collect and copy all the Latin inscriptions in existence. Working for more than a quarter of a century under his directing genius, they built up a collection covering many thousands of inscriptions, arranged in about forty huge tomes with superb indices—one of the greatest monuments of historical investigation ever created. Mommsen himself declared: "Scholarship suffers from waste of energy, as a plant suffers from a worm at its root. The remedy is organization and concentration." It is worth noting that he was born in a poor and lonely parsonage where he saw little of any other children except his two brothers and one sister, that he was educated at home by his father, and that he did not go to school until he was

---

*R. Pfeiffer, *History of Classical Scholarship* (Oxford, 1968), Part 2, esp. cc. 1 and 4.

†K. Zangemeister's list of Mommsen's published works, completed by E. Jacobs in *Theodor Mommsen als Schriftsteller* (Berlin, 1905), runs to 1,513 items: a few trifles, many masterworks.

nearly seventeen. There, however, he joined a classicists' club, and realized for the first time (in his own words) that "men polish each other as diamonds do." When he became chairman of the little club he made a speech which contained a firm statement of the rule he followed throughout his career: *"Immer strebe zum Ganzen!"* "Work always toward completeness!"

Closely allied to this intellectual ideal is a fourth principle of scholarship. I write of it with some diffidence, because I have seldom been able to apply it. This is *collaboration.* Forty or fifty years ago (in the field I know best) a book would come out with one author's name, and with few if any acknowledgments—except to institutions of learning—in the preface. Now it is the accepted thing, particularly in Britain, for the author to thank three colleagues and friends for reading his book *in typescript,* two more for reading it *in proof,* and four or five others for discussing individual chapters with him after they were drafted. The result of this practice has been to raise the standards of scholarly precision very considerably, and, I believe, to engage scholars more deeply in their work.

Not only that. We have all known colleagues who, although learned and diligent, have been unable to put their learning down on paper. They always want to do a little more research before committing themselves, to rethink their interpretation of two or three major problems, to wait until somebody else's book appears, or to postpone writing until the blessed sabbatical arrives. Such men have a block. Sometimes collaboration with another scholar can make the block disappear. The two partners meet regularly. Each feels he must produce something for the other to work with. A plan which frightens or discourages one man can easily be carried out by two. The drudgery, through being shared, diminishes. Each, from his experience, suggests methods which the other had not thought of. In such a case, two heads are ten times better than one.

No doubt there are exceptions: lonely geniuses such as Isaac Newton. He was twenty-two, living in a remote Lincolnshire village without intellectual companionship, when he worked out the binomial theorem, the principle of integral calculus, the composition of light, and the gravitational explanation of the motions of the moon. For such a man, you might think, scholarly collaboration must be unfruitful or impracticable; and indeed he himself, when first invited to join the Royal Society, wrote in an immortal phrase that he was "reluctant to extend the circle of his acquaintance." And yet some of Newton's good work was done under the stimulus of criticism from Hooke, and some in response to the admiration and encouragement of Halley. These and other such men were in a certain sense Newton's collaborators. An incident from his later life illustrates this. The Swiss mathematician Jakob Bernoulli published two problems, and defied anyone in the scientific world to solve them within six months. Newton solved them both within twenty-four hours. His challenger was his collaborator.

The life of learning has many more ideals: some of them more difficult to define than these, and more difficult to attain. There is the gift of *interpretation*, which enables people from one culture to understand the inhabitants of another and alien culture. As a classicist I often envy a professor of Japanese in an American university, who can talk with a professor of American and English literature in a Japanese university, and I wish that I could just spend a few hours with an ancient Greek or Roman scholar: even a morning in the Museum of Alexandria. In those few hours I could clear up twenty questions that have bothered me for fifty years. There is also the priceless gift of hermeneutics, *discovery*, by which a few of us are enabled to locate and explore new fields of inquiry, to connect hitherto isolated data and give them fresh significance, to devise novel investigative methods which solve hitherto intractable problems. To possess and exercise that gift is the highest reward of the creative scholar.

Difficult and demanding, the principles of learning. But what of the principles of teaching?

They are different: occasionally they seem to conflict with the principles of scholarship.

For example, should a teacher manifest *humility*? Toward his subject, yes. Toward his pupils, certainly not. He knows far more than they do; and he usually works much harder. It is not uncommon nowadays, before a doctoral defense, to receive a dissertation which has been so carelessly written and proofread by the candidate that the examiner is forced to spend several hours checking and altering false references and correcting both spelling and punctuation. When you have to do such donkey-work for a student aspiring to the highest academic degree, you know very well who is the donkey, and you do not feel constrained to humility in his presence. No: the difficulty is to find a middle way, between decent modesty and necessary authority. Arrogance is always wrong. We should not think that teaching means "casting sham pearls before real swine." Or at least we should never say so.

As you grow older and presumably more distinguished, your relation with your students changes. Although inevitable, this is sometimes disconcerting; but you must adapt yourself to the change. Mannerisms and attitudes which were appropriate to a man or woman of thirty are usually quite inappropriate when he or she has turned fifty. I still recall attending a lecture course on an important and difficult theme: the *Republic* of Plato. The lecturer used no notes, seldom glanced at the text, and delivered his informal, almost shapeless disquisitions, not standing at a lectern or pacing the platform, but perching jauntily on a table and swinging his legs. All right, perhaps, if he had been a brilliant youngster on whom informality sat well. But he was pudgy and balding and well over fifty years of age. It was impossible for the young to respect him: it was difficult even to listen to him with concentration. As he grew older, he should have modified his manner, and adapted it to the change in his age relationship with his students; and so must we all.

Devotion to the subject is the one factor which inspires both sound learning and sound teaching. If one is really keen on a discipline, one's enthusiasm will usually communicate itself to the students. Even if they do not share it (perhaps because they find the subject itself dull and repellent) they will at least become aware of the wider possibilities of intellectual adventure. Some years ago several Vassar girls published a delightful book of drawings poking gentle fun at life in Vassar. One showed a

small class of flowerlike young creatures (this was before
the days of bare feet and dirty hair), dutiful and beautiful, listening in half-embarrassed astonishment while an
elderly professor, raising her arms to the ceiling in ecstasy, cried: "Oh, girls, is it not truly marvelous to hear
the echo of a single vowel ringing down the centuries!"
Now, one of the miracles of language is just the intricate
development of a single word or even a single sound,
from its dark origins far away and long ago, through
many different societies and at last into the languages of
other groups than its first users; and one of the great
achievements of modern linguistics is the subtlety and
skill with which it can trace that process. But it is a tough
and highly technical subject. The girls found the lectures
on linguistics arid as well as difficult; none of them felt
she might devote the rest of her life to the study of the
sounds of language. At that age they could not understand why anyone should carry on such research not
only as a professional duty but as a pleasure. I enjoy
playing chess and appreciate Fischer's ambition to be the
Master of the (Chess) World; but I find it hard to understand how André Chéron could build an entire career on
studying the end-game. Still, they saw that the old lady
had found happiness, rich positive delight, in exercising
her *mind*; and long after they had forgotten all about the
Great Vowel Shift they would remember her ecstasy,
perhaps even, in another intellectual field, reexperience
it for themselves. They may not have become acolytes,
but they had been set on the road toward conversion.

One warning. Devotion to a field in the world of scholarship sometimes involves hatred of one's rivals. This
should be excluded from lectures and from discussions
with students—except, just conceivably, on the level of

a graduate seminar. To tell a captive audience how your last book was scalped and mutilated by a personal enemy, or to hang up the effigy of an absent scholar and shoot burning arrows at it, may relieve your own feelings, but will surely alienate the young people.

As a naïve but enthusiastic young freshman, I was in a large class reading the comedies of the Latin poet Terence. The language of the plays was not difficult; the style was brisk and elegant. But several things puzzled us all. The plays were written in Latin for a Roman audience: so why were all their characters and settings Greek? Why were the plots so infernally complicated? And above all, why weren't they *funny*? The comedies we saw at the movies were full of jokes. We had read some Shakespeare at school, and remembered from his comedies droll characters like Pistol and Malvolio; but we found scarcely anyone like that in Terence. Now, all these questions ought to have been taken up by our professor, J.S. Phillimore. He ignored them. He made his way scene by scene through the plays, translating and elucidating very gracefully; but from time to time he stopped to pour scorn on someone whom he called "the man Fleckeisen." None of us dared to ask him who Fleckeisen was. Much later I discovered that he was a German scholar who, thirty or forty years earlier, had made a lot of daring and foolish conjectures on the text of Terence; but frankly, as a freshman straight from school, I did not even know that the printed words in front of me were not the single authentic version, but were put together from various different manuscripts. Now, Phillimore could easily have led us into a discussion of how and why ancient manuscripts differ from one another; how a scholar goes about constructing from them a readable and sensible text to send to the printer;

and exactly what was wrong with the methods of Fleck-eisen. No doubt this would have taken us off Terence's comedies for an hour or two, but it would have sharpened our critical perceptions and enlarged our intellectual horizons. But no. All we got was pointless vituperation of "the man Fleckeisen."

Furthermore, the interests of the students are more widely diffused than yours. Their attention is still divided between the academic cosmos and the larger world of money-making, social maladjustment, and political strife. Before they come to class, they have read the papers or at least heard the radio. They have been told about a race riot, a gigantic financial swindle, a guerrilla war. If they see you getting excited because one of your pet theories has been hamstrung by somebody they have never heard of, they will certainly respect you no more than before, and may lose some of their concern for the subject you are trying to teach them.

Love of one's subject is best shown through constant intellectual *renewal*. The young are narrow-minded. The young are short-sighted. They cannot, without an exceptional effort, conceive how large and complex an important intellectual discipline is, what a wealth of material and multiplicity of problems it embodies; the teaching they get in high school tends to make them superficial, and to suggest to them that arduous, long-term thinking and research are not necessary for higher mental achievement; they are bombarded by the outer world with trivial novelties in news, fashions, and entertainment; their inner life is distorted by the temptations of sex and drugs; and they tend to believe that we, their teachers, are "set in our ways" and go placidly on doing the same sort of nothing year after year.

It is our duty, therefore, indeed it is one of our chief

functions as teachers, to show them that the world of the intellect is in constant flux, that our own minds are always meeting and grappling with new challenges, and that the most important part of our work is discovery and reinterpretation. A colleague tells me that he recently handed out a set of bibliographies dealing solely with new and stimulating articles in specialist periodicals—the periodicals which our students seldom read until they approach the Ph.D. degree: sometimes not even then; not even later. He ran through the titles, telling the young people what problem each article raised and how it was handled.

Silence. Astonishment.

Then one of them asked for more of the same, with the significant remark: "I never knew there was so much going on!" They had assumed that the world of scholarship was static or moribund, like those stars called "white dwarfs" which gleam faintly before they become dead, ice-covered dots; and that we ourselves, if not dead, were at least cataleptic. Not so. Ours is a lively world, ringing with conflicts and buzzing with problems. One of the central principles governing both our teaching and our learning is incessant *renewal*. After a long career of strife and accomplishment, the first great Athenian, Solon, said that his last years were governed by this rule:

I grow old learning much and always learning.

THE
NEED FOR
RENEWAL

When I started teaching, I thought it would become easier as I went along. Now I know it does not. In one way teaching as a profession is scarcely comparable to medicine or the church. After twenty years' experience a doctor knows an enlarged spleen when he feels one, and a priest or minister knows what to say to a mourner or a sinner; but the average teacher has no such thorough grasp of his craft, because it is constantly changing and he himself must change with it. Perhaps teaching should rather be compared with the arts—or else with the most difficult and unrewarding of all occupations, politics. In Winston Churchill's memoirs one of the most noteworthy points is that, in spite of half a century's experience and a vast knowledge of history, Churchill never felt he could find a permanent answer to any problem. He could only produce temporary solutions; and hope for the best. That is true for teachers also. No solution to any of our problems is permanent. Change and renewal are constantly necessary. We must incessantly reexamine our job and ourselves.

To begin with, the subjects we teach keep changing. There is hardly a single subject that remains static except on the most elementary level. Consider the new theories about the life and work of Shakespeare that have been put forward recently; consider the sinister revelations about the life and death of Christopher Marlowe. Any teacher of English literature must know these novelties and bring them into his teaching. For historians it is now mandatory to explain the Marxist conception of history, and to show where and how far it is wrong. The young are going to come into contact with it, and it is therefore our duty to give them a clear, analytic view of its powers and weaknesses. Not long ago, geography used to be one of the dullest and most mechanically taught subjects in school. Gloomily do I recall spending hours on mapping the innumerable islands and lochs of the western coasts of Scotland, in four colors, with a set of fine draftsman's instruments; and memorizing the exports of the South American republics, most of which seemed to consist of "coffee and cinchona." But now we all travel a hundred times oftener and farther than our parents did; we worry about the use and abuse of the land and the sea; we have learned the strategic importance of certain tiny patches of territory in war past or future; the oceans have been fought over like land battlefields, and will soon be harvested and quarried like the solid earth; the Antarctic continent has been added to our horizon; we are even beginning to think about invading the interior of the planet. Now geography is an important branch of knowledge, essential in every school and university.

Again, whether we know it or not, our attitude toward our material changes. We emphasize one part of it and we rather neglect the rest; or we increase our interest in research and diminish our investment in teaching; or else we take on more and more pupils and offer more courses and abandon our research "until things get straightened out around here," i.e., never. We can also be sidetracked into administrative functions. I remember wasting three entire weeks on preparing a budgetary projection to cover the next five years—a plan which was rendered completely meaningless by unforeseen and unforeseeable events. Or sometimes we augment our own knowledge so that we know too much to teach. Several distinguished scholars who are immersed in large and important subjects suffer from this hypertrophy. If a well-informed person asks them penetrating questions about their field, they will reply freely; but if they have to talk about it to laymen or beginning students, they have scarcely any idea where to begin, because the whole thing seems equally important and familiar to them. They know it all; but they do not know what other people do not know about it.

Sometimes we are disappointed or bored. If a book of ours meets with failure or we are denied promotion, we are apt to lose heart: usually the depression comes on us unawares, so that until three or four years have passed, we scarcely notice that we have become sour and crabby to the pupils and colleagues we used to like. Very often a young man who is good in a big institution, surrounded by competitors and constantly stimulated, moves to a smaller one, and there becomes lazy or stupid; very often a young woman who is good in a small institution moves to a big one, and grows shy and nervous, taciturn and retiring; very often an older colleague on whom a young teacher has been depending will move away or retire or die, and then the teacher's life flattens out and loses force. As we grow older, too, we begin to realize that—while comparatively dull men who were classmates of ours are now senior partners and managing directors and ambassadors, and go to work in chauffeured limousines—we ourselves shall never be rich, or even comfortably well off. Against such disappointments we must be constantly on our guard. It is our duty to face them and overcome them, by regularly renewed moral strength.

Occasionally we grow discouraged because we have to repeat the same material again and again. For this there are two solutions. One is expressed in Ezra Pound's phrase MAKE IT NEW. Brisken up the course. Bring in novel illustrations. Approach it from a fresh point of view. Invite a visitor to teach one class. Read controversial discussions of problems in the subject, assimilate them, and introduce them to your pupils. Whenever a good new book in the field comes out, digest it and it will give you more vitality than a shot of B_{12}. The other solution is to remember that you are not repeating, but creating. Every time a teacher faces a class, he or she is creating something which did not exist before. Even if the pupils always belong to the same age group and social milieu, every class is an entity different from other classes in the past, every pupil in it is a novelty, and the whole thing is a new opportunity.

Again, our relationship to our pupils changes from one year to another. At the age of forty-five, you cannot teach in the same way as you did when you were twenty-five. You see the students differently. You look different to them. Once upon a time, perhaps, you might even have been mistaken for one of their group. Later, and not too much later, the generations leave you behind, and you begin to seem like an uncle or an aunt, a father or a mother, a judge or a head nurse. Accept this change, and be prepared for its continuance.

Another aspect of this particular problem is that our own intellectual control grows firmer year by year. Most teachers are mentally mature, and can grasp complex themes firmly and thoroughly. But the young do not. They cannot. As our control grows firmer, we tend to forget how difficult it is for them and to despise them for failing to understand. This is a serious mistake. By definition, our pupils are immature, and our chief duty is not to scorn them for their inability to comprehend, but to help them in overcoming their weakness. Or, to put it another way, our grasp of our subject matter is apt to become automatic—so that we assume far too much knowledge in the young. An English teacher might well be horrified and disgusted if one of his pupils betrayed that he thought Chaucer was a contemporary of Shakespeare. Anyone who knows English literature associates Chaucer with the late fourteenth century and Shakespeare with the late sixteenth century: Chaucer with the Middle Ages, Shakespeare with the High Renaissance. But that is not at all so obvious to a youngster who sees portraits of both poets wearing what seem to him to be "historical" clothes and who finds their works close to each other in the school library. It is our duty to assume that nothing is known, and to explain everything clearly and without condescension. The students are eternally young: it is we who change, and we must adapt ourselves to them as the years pass. There is one stylistic development which most people seldom notice in themselves or others, but which should be watched. As we grow older, we use more and more abstract nouns and adjectives: we move up the semantic ladder. The man who at twenty-five would have said: "Tough nut to crack," will when he is fifty-five say: "Conceivably that might be a problem which admits no solution." Watch the young carefully as you talk. When you use words such as *stylistic development* and *abstract* and *semantic* and *anomalous* and *abrogate* and its illegitimate brother *surrogate* and *modality* and so forth—particularly if you cluster them closely together—you can observe the eyes of your students growing lightly glazed, as though you were brushing them over with warm aspic. Much as I admire T.S. Eliot's poems, I fear that his prose criticism makes me yawny and dozy, for this same reason; and his famous phrase *the objective correlative* sends me right off into a peaceful nap. We must always watch our pupils, always striving to discern their interest or lack of interest. By their faces one can tell whether they are following or not. Rapport is essential. (That sentence, *Rapport is essential*, would lose about 30 percent of the average class.)

Sometimes I wonder if teaching is like golf—a succession of bad habits, successively corrected. In golf you develop a slice, so that your drives all curve away out to the right and land in rough territory. Slowly and painfully you correct it (turning the left hand farther round, and following through more consistently). By the time it has been cured, your short iron shots have gone to hell. With a good deal of practice you make them deft and neat, but now the putting has deteriorated and the ball will not go into the little hole on the smooth grass surface. After a few days of intensive putting you become quite passable on the greens, but you have now started shanking every tenth shot away off into the boondocks. It seems to be the same with teaching. There are no permanent solutions. There are no permanent solutions; but we must not be discouraged.

Then again, the pupils change in many ways. Not, of course, in their youth and immaturity, but in their attitudes to education and to the world. The most obvious change is that caused by the thought of war. In the Humanities course at Columbia College we begin with Homer's *Iliad*. The earliest, and in some ways the greatest, poem in European literature, this epic is wholly devoted to war, covering almost every aspect of it: violence, cruelty, waste, madness, suffering, self-sacrifice, nobility, and heroism. In the years before World War II it was very hard to teach the *Iliad*. Some of the young men could scarcely compel themselves to read it because of savage scenes like this, from the exploits of Achilles (20.474–483):

> He struck Agenor's son Echeclus
> right through the head with his strong hilted
>   sword,
> and all the sword grew hot with blood: Echeclus'
>   eyes
> were gripped fast by dark death and powerful
>   doom.
> Then next Deucalion, where the nerves and
>   muscles join
> at the elbow, there he stabbed him through the arm
> with a bronze spear. Deucalion stood there
>   crippled,
> face to face with death. Achilles, striking his neck,

drove head and helmet far away: out of the
    backbone
the marrow gushed, and he fell prostrate on the
    earth.

Others, who compelled themselves to complete the as-
signment and went through the whole epic, twenty-four
books of bloodshed and agony, could not see why it
should be called a great poem, since it dealt with such a
revolting subject. Long and tactful discussion was required before they would approach it as a work of art.
With Jews, Bible-reading Protestants, and Mormons, it
was sometimes helpful to compare Homer's battle scenes
with those in the Old Testament—even more bloody
though less detailed—such as the victories recorded in
Joshua (chapters 6, 8, 10, 11) and the battles of David (e.g.,
1 Samuel 27, 2 Samuel 8); but the class as a whole was
never at ease.

A few years later, however, the returning veterans of
World War II tackled the *Iliad* with zest, contributing
realistic comments from their own experiences, and ap-
preciating many aspects of the poem which had been lost
on previous generations of students. With one group I
began a discussion by asking: "You know what the main
plot is, don't you? A dispute between the supreme com-
mander Agamemnon and his finest fighter Achilles, over
a girl. (What's the girl's name again? Briseis, right, thank
you, Lenahan.) Now, the two men are not in love with
her. This is not a love-triangle: we'll get that in Shakespeare's *Troilus and Cressida*. It is a matter of prestige. By
taking away his loot, his prize of honor, from Achilles,
Agamemnon has insulted him. Now, have you all got
that?" I was ready for an argument or for further expla-

nations; but they said: "Right, sir, go ahead." Lenahan added: "Whenever we took a village in the Philippines, the top brass got first choice of the women." Thenceforward we moved smoothly through the *Iliad*; and the freshmen who instead of being veterans had come straight from high school to college got a surprising but invaluable double education in literature and life.

A month or two later we tackled Aristotle's *Ethics*. This book contains, among other things, the curious theory that virtue is often not the opposite of vice, but is rather the happy medium between two extremes, both faulty—one an excess and the other a deficiency. It is impossible to use this theory for such acts as theft or murder (as Aristotle himself admits) but can it be applied, for example, to courage?* Is courage not the opposite of cowardice? Is a coward not simply a man who lacks some important quality, and if so how can there be anyone who has too much of that quality? Yet Aristotle declares firmly that courage is halfway between two extremes. One is cowardice. The other is rashness. Both are wrong. I asked the class whether they thought this was true. After a meditative silence, Lenahan said: "When we were on patrol in the jungle, there was one guy in the platoon who always held a grenade with the pin already pulled, so that he could throw it in half a second if something came up. We thought he was off his trolley, just as badly as if he'd been crawling along on his belly, crying."

Some years passed. There was the Korean War; then the Vietnam War. Once more it became excessively diffi-

---

*Aristotle's discussion of this is in *Nicomachean Ethics* 3.7; there is a good translation by J.A.K. Thomson (Penguin Books, 1955).

cult to discuss the *Iliad* in class; and even toward Vergil's *Aeneid*, in which war is described less extensively and with far less gusto, students were unsympathetic or hostile. Finally came the student disorders of 1968 and subsequent years, not only in the United States, but in France and Japan, Italy and Mexico, England and Argentina— a worldwide phenomenon as difficult to understand as the outbreak of a new epidemic disease, and for most teachers impossible at first to confront without intense spiritual pain, which sometimes developed into contempt or alienation or hostility. Here the teacher's main duty was to maintain the high standards of his profession: dispassionate fairness, steady pursuit of knowledge, strong but sympathetic control of his classes, and confident self-discipline. Those teachers who behaved like this vindicated themselves, and set an example both to their weaker colleagues and to the excited and irrational students—an example to be remembered after the spiritual temperature of schools and universities returns to normal.

The technique of propaganda is developing very fast. We must expect the young to be affected by it far more than they realize: as a physician in Tokyo or Los Angeles nowadays, when examining a patient with malaise and low vitality, always suspects lung damage because of the foulness of the air. In 1920 or 1930 one could attend school and college without having heard much propaganda, or, because it was the crude type employed by press barons like Hearst and Beaverbrook, without having one's mind disturbed by it.* Nowadays, however, we are given hun-

---

*Exception: the subtle communist propaganda injected into a few selected victims at Oxford and Cambridge, which produced the trai-

dreds of doses of propaganda every week, some violent
and disturbing like the hate sheets dealing with the problems of race, some quiet and insidious and all but imper-
ceptible, designed to have their ultimate effect years or
decades later. Students are preconditioned. They are
supplied with prejudices (which they do not admit to be
prejudices) and assumptions (which they will not analyse
and will not permit others to analyse) covering a large
number of general problems. This makes it far more
difficult today for a teacher to give instruction or conduct a discussion on any subject which is or can be made
controversial. More difficult, not because the pupils are
silent, dull, obstinate, impercipient—which is a desperate situation for any teacher—but because so much time
and energy must be spent in destroying misconceptions
and exposing falsehoods and shredding waste intellectual material. So much patience and forbearance are required that a teacher who has a strong personality and
knows what he is talking about may find it hard not to
flash out, like Prospero to his daughter Miranda: "What?
My foot my tutor?"* The young are delighted to debate
on controversial subjects, but (unknown to themselves)
they do not approach them with truly open minds. This
may be why so many have joined quasi-religious sects
which teach their adherents to do "transcendental medi-
tation," which means freeing the mind and washing the
brain clean.

The communities which feed schools and colleges
have never been stable. Recently there have been two

tors Philby, Burgess, and Maclean, as well as others, not all of them
yet known.
* *The Tempest* I, ii, 466.

chief difficulties arising from community changes: larger and larger classes in rooms which seem to grow smaller and dirtier, and the irruption of many pupils who present grave problems of assimilation, either because they come from homes where English is not spoken, or because they are affected by hostility between groups. In many countries of the world, the teacher seems to be the representative of the established order, opposed to the aspirations of the revolutionary proletariat, and therefore to be a fascist beast whose authority must be rejected; in other lands, the teacher, underpaid and socially disinherited, is a natural apostle of rebellion, producing generation after generation of explosive young revolutionaries. In the United States the central issue seems to be one of adjustment between teachers who belong to the white-European and old-line–American tradition, and pupils who are not white and who identify themselves with underprivileged colored peoples all over the world.

One central problem, particularly painful, is that of teaching Negro children to read and write. The militant Negro leader Huey P. Newton says in his autobiography* that in high school he simply rejected the idea of learning these skills, necessary though they are, because he loathed the ordeal of being taught by a white teacher: since, in order to learn, he would have had to accept direction and to do exercises ("taking orders") and to admit inferiority to the white man or woman who knew more than he did. (Eventually, he asserts, he was taught by one of his brothers.) But there may be other reasons for the fact that many Negro children find reading and writing very hard to learn: one of them that they talk and

------

*Revolutionary Suicide (New York, 1973).

think in their own special dialect, so that when given a book written in standard American they are repelled by it as unfamiliar, over-complicated, almost foreign. This point is made sympathetically by Peter Farb in *Word Play.** He outlines the distinctive pronunciation and grammar of what he calls "Black English," and goes on:

> Most school systems are unaware that lower-class black children enter the first grade speaking a mother dialect that is not Standard English. The exasperated white teacher, who knows little about Black English, usually concludes that the black child is unteachable, because he refuses to learn to read simple English. The teacher reprimands the black child for saying *they toys* and *he work* when he clearly sees printed in his reader *their toys* and *he's working.* . . . Often black teachers themselves are the worst offenders in stigmatizing Black English. Obviously they view as inferior that speech which they worked so hard to unlearn in themselves.

For schools and colleges the problem of the changing community is the largest, and therefore the most difficult to solve. Probably no single solution is possible for all its variations. But one general rule is always valid. Teachers are not expected to change as rapidly as other elements of society: they should not. Like the churches and the doctors, they are anchors in the midst of a tempestuous sea of change. They provide stability, they provide a sense of tradition, they represent a code of manners and of sensibilities. Against them the young can test their

---

*New York, 1974: chapter 7.

numerous experiments, many of which they will find foolish and shallow. But without the firm, confident durability of the teachers, many of the main values of civilization will very quickly disappear into chaos. In the epoch we live in, change is an ideal for its own sake; and this ideal—at least in human terms—is mistaken or painfully exaggerated and overprized. The central conditions of human happiness and human excellence and human morality are not about to be altered, either in this generation or in the next ten generations. This we should remember. On this we should insist.

The last of these problems is the fact that we all grow older. Physical strength, or at least physical durability, is a great help in teaching; but after the age of forty-five or so it diminishes rapidly. And further, every ten or fifteen years, the young seem to grow larger: certainly taller, often if not always stronger, and therefore physically more difficult to meet on equal terms. The process of aging affects one's health, and with it one's attitude to the surrounding world. If one feels one's heart overtaxed or one's sight deteriorating, it is far more difficult to be polite to a young healthy pupil who asks a stupid question. As the old man says in Terence's comedy: "old age is itself a disease."* The same problem confronts all sensitive people: poets and musicians, who are often afraid that they may have written themselves out. Wordsworth, after experiencing such a crisis of depression, composed a poem about it, and summed it up in an immortal image.

----

*Phormio 575: senectus ipsast morbus.

The Youth, who daily farther from the east
Must travel, still is Nature's priest,
  And by the vision splendid
  Is on his way attended.
At length the Man perceives it die away,
And fade into the light of common day.*

Are there any consolations for the slowing of our impetus, for the diminution of our strength? Yes, a few. As we age, we acquire better balance, better stability. When I was more vigorous, it was a constant effort of will for me to stay at the desk long enough to finish a long, tiresome job. Now I can do it, because as my muscles have grown less full of electricity my will power has strengthened. Again, the onset of old age is at least retarded for most teachers by their association with the young. Not one of us is mature all through, or thoroughly old: in all of us there remains an element of youth, which enjoys mixing with, or at least looking at and listening to, young people, and helps to keep us younger. Finally, as we grow older, we understand our own subject better, we understand our pupils better, and we have a stronger appreciation of the long history of scholarship and teaching that sustains us. Experience as a teacher and scholar is not to be built up within a few years. It is the achievement of many long energetic seasons of grappling with a wide diversity of problems. When we grow older, it is part of our reward. The remainder of that reward is the knowledge that, within all this change, we are maintaining the long, magnificent tradition of creative teaching.

---

*Ode, *Intimations of Immortality*, v.

TEACHING
COLLEGE
TEACHERS
HOW TO TEACH

This is a tricky problem. Men and women who are going to teach school children are elaborately trained in educational techniques and the psychology of the young and many other skills. On these they spend much time and effort; and even if (after passing their examinations) they retain very little in precise detail, they are at least convinced that *how* they teach is as important as *what* they teach. But men and women destined to teach in colleges and universities seldom receive any formal training of that kind. Many begin by teaching badly out of sheer inexperience. Some continue to teach badly all their lives long. It makes them unhappy, with a dull, persistent ache; and meanwhile, year after year, "the hungry sheep look up, and are not fed."

The problem has two horns. One is straight and sharp: what is a young Ph.D. to be taught about teaching? The other is blunt and twisted: how, when, and by whom is he to be taught?

To begin with, at the outset of their career, young Ph.D.'s must learn, must really be convinced, that teaching well is an imperative duty. It is absolutely *necessary* for them. Unless they are fortunate enough to be invited to join the Institute for Advanced Study at Princeton or some other center of pure research, they will be teaching all through their active lives. It is an obligation they cannot escape and can only at their own serious risk evade. If they do not recognize this and accept it, they will teach as a disagreeable chore, face their students with a perceptible grudge, and inevitably grow into those embittered and harsh teachers whom we all, from our own youthful times, remember with distaste. It is grand to do keen research, to make discoveries, to plunge deeper and deeper into a fascinating subject. Yet very few colleges and universities can afford to support men and women who devote their lives to nothing but pure scholarship, never leaving their laboratory benches or their carrels in the library. It is not solely a matter of money. Students have recently grown more vocal about their grievances (real or fancied) and more active in protesting against what they consider to be abuses in university life. Bitterly, they often say they feel hurt and deprived when they know a distinguished scholar is working in the same institution, but can never hear him talk or benefit from his learning. They feel this even if they could no more understand his disquisitions than I could understand a symposium on quantum mechanics. Like pious Hindus with a saint, they do not necessarily want to touch him or hear his speeches, but to get *darshan*, the mystical joy of communion, from his nearness. The dedicated researcher may also offend and alienate his own colleagues. Even if he works nine hours a day six days a week, bringing fame not only to himself but to his department, still, when they, not he, have to do the donkey-work of reading masters' essays and giving mid-term and final examinations, they will resent it. They will even begrudge him the distinction which he wins, for they will feel that they had to work hard and neglect their own projects in order to make it possible. Unjust, no doubt; but human.

The newly fledged Ph.D. must understand that teaching is really necessary for the students: active, energetic teaching. Sometimes he or she does not really believe this. He—I wish there were a handy neutral pronoun meaning "he or she": "one" does not always fit—he (or she) was often a bookworm or a laboratory wizard from early youth. In his heart he believes that anyone can learn anything by dogged application. *There is the apparatus. Perform the experiment in the prescribed stages. These are the required books. Read them diligently, and you will understand them just as I did at your age. What is the obstacle?* It is this belief that misleads some beginning teachers into a dismal tactical mistake: instead of giving, in their own words with the force of their own personality behind it, the essence of a historical explanation or of a literary analysis, they will read aloud long passages from printed books, and thus dilute the whole force of their teaching and dilute their authority. Ph.D.'s are exceptional people. Therefore they must allow for minds which are less keen, less confident, less well prepared than theirs—or poorly adjusted or hampered by unseen and sometimes undiagnosable blockages. I myself speak French and German fairly fluently and without embarrassment, having learned them both when young. But I always have to make an effort to realize that a friend of mine, whom I know to be versatile and intelligent, simply cannot bring himself to pronounce sounds which are not native to his own language. He will never be able to say *Goethe* or *hors d'oeuvres* because of their half-open front vowel, or *Rue de la Paix* and *Kurfürstendamm* because of that narrow *u*. He does not believe that such noises exist, or at least that he ought to try to make them. I remember once rescuing an old English lady from a Parisian taxi driver whom she was denouncing with righteous indignation. (The English specialize in righteous indignation.) "Noolie, Noolie!" she cried, and was very angry when he shrugged his shoulders and spread his hands and shook his head. Fortunately she had the address written down, and when she showed it to me I told the driver she wanted to go to the suburb called Neuilly. There are four sounds in N-eu-ill-y (maybe even four and a half), and she had got only one of them right. Like my friend Mike Monoglot, she had a block which kept her from trying to imitate foreign noises.

Many students, far more than college and university teachers realize, have emotional and intellectual impediments, often without knowing it themselves; and one of the imperative duties of teachers is to diminish or remove them. Furthermore, many students do not really know how to study. Their parents never opened a book (and secretly were afraid of books). Their home was full of family disorder, whether jolly and stimulating or self-poisoning and sick. Their schooling was slack and undisciplined. Such youths and girls can scarcely bring themselves to believe two essential truths: first, that reading a book is an activity almost as natural as talking or listening to music; second, that without mental effort and concentration they will never achieve anything in adult life, and the plain, necessary jobs, like keeping the household budget and watching the savings account and filling in tax forms and planning for the happiness of their families, all will be hideous torments to be avoided, or even, out of nausea and spite, mishandled and bungled. A couple of generations ago discipline in many families and schools was too severe. Now it has become too slack, and it is producing a multitude of Dharma bums and layabouts, whose ideal of living is to jump in a car like Kerouac, and take off—for where?

> One moment in Annihilation's Waste,
> One moment, of the Well of Life to taste—
> The Stars are setting, and the Caravan
> Starts for the Dawn of Nothing—Oh, make haste!

Fitzgerald's verses make it sound urgent; it is the pure doctrine of the Cyrenaics, that the pleasure of each instant is the sole end of life; but it is false. As the moment repeats itself, and the repeated moments lengthen out into months, and the months to years, and the years toward a lifetime, sooner or later (sometimes too late) everyone discovers it is false: that forethought, and order, and preparation, and planning, and self-control, and self-discipline are necessary for anyone who hopes for durable happiness.

A good teacher teaches not only his own subject, but also the principles of study and concentration—and their rewards. Dull or distracted youngsters have to be shown these matters in detail. Bright ones find out for themselves. When I was engaged with the Humanities course at Columbia, dealing with the great books, a freshman came to see me and ask for advice. At first he had been overwhelmed by the difficulty and complexity and strangeness of Homer's *Iliad* and Aeschylus' *Prometheus Bound* and Herodotus' *History*. He wanted help in approaching these books and the others, all so different, all masterpieces. They were marvelous, he told me, but he was not accustomed to having his mind stretched like this. That is real education, I told him, having your mind stretched and at the same time made more supple; and I gave him some encouragement and some hints. Much relieved, he rose to go. Then: "Why should I be finding this so tough?" he asked. I said: "This time last year, in November, what were you doing in high school? what took up most of your time and energy?" "Last year," he said; "oh, I was managing the football team." Great fun, no doubt; but he was not learning how to use his mind. Several years later, when he was a senior with a good record behind him and a good career ahead of him, he told me he still felt bitter about the years he had squandered in high school.

The young Ph.D. must realize that teaching is actually good for him or her. It helps his private research in several ways. New problems are posed to him by the questions of his pupils. If they are too shy or too torpid to ask him questions orally, it is his duty to stimulate them into argument—if not with him, then with one another. And a careful reading of their examination papers will always produce material for discussion: misunderstandings (due either to their misreading of a book or to his own maladroit teaching) to be clarified, misinterpretations (produced by bias or inadequate information) to be corrected, strong conflicts of opinion to be impartially stated and analyzed. Again, he will often find that hypotheses he himself had always accepted without reflection strike his students as unnecessary or fantastic. Gaps in his knowledge will appear: he must go to the sources and remedy the deficiency. If he is wise, he will admit that he does not know the answer right away; and then, having discovered it, he will frankly tell his pupils how and where he found the solution.

And of course everyone—everyone except a few favored by nature—needs practice in speaking and writing. A bad talker will nearly always be a bad writer too. It is easy, sometimes painfully easy, to detect when you are not communicating your thoughts to a class. Try again. Restate the ideas. Run them over at home. Shape them differently, alter the emphasis, add a vivid illustration, coin (or steal) a few epigrams to enliven them; even put them on tape and play them back to your own ears. Sometimes you will be surprised at what comes out of the recording machine. Once I had a colleague who used the "hesitation monosyllable" at least once or twice in every—er—sentence. It was—er—impossible, quite impossible (for he used emphatic repetition too), for him to make even a short—er—statement without an agonizing —er—pause. As he grew older and more distinguished (for he was a notable scholar), his voice became firmer and more authoritative. But so did his—ER—hesitations, they blared out like trombones. It was—ER, ER—weird to watch him talking, and to see that, every time he made that disgusting noise, his expression did not alter in the least. He was absolutely unconscious of it: it was as natural to him as his breathing or the movement of his eyelids; and yet one could stand outside the closed door of a lecture room and at once detect that it was he, and no other, who was addressing a class inside. His ERs made the very windows rattle. Everyone is disconcerted when he first hears his own voice on tape. It is certain that, if my colleague had ever been taped and had heard the playback, he would have been horrified by this habit, and tried hard to erase and eradicate the error.

You know, the teachers' colleges are not always wrong. One point they do well to insist on is motivation. To teach well in college or university, the new graduate must have a strong sense of purpose. Motivation. . . . The word feels too weak. May we not say *dedication*?

Young Ph.D.'s newly graduated sometimes think it is enough to know something about their subject and then start talking about it. Not so. Their students have to learn the subject from them, it is true. But they ought also to learn intellectual control. Most uneducated and half-educated men and women do not comprehend aesthetic and logical structures. They cannot see a long book or a big topic as a whole made up of interrelated parts. Their attention spans are short: their powers of large-scale understanding are embryonic.

To take an easy example, millions of people have studied the Bible, but very few of them have ever tried to analyze it. Partly this is because the language (except in a few modern translations) and the thought patterns are strange and difficult; partly because they feel it inappropriate to apply logic to a holy book; partly, if they are very pious, because they believe it to be the word of God, which must be accepted as flawlessly perfect even when it incorporates what look like inconsistencies; but partly too because, being divided (not always logically) into chapters and verse, the Bible is hard to see as a whole or a set of wholes. Right at the beginning of the first book there are two separate and different accounts of the creation of the world. The first covers Genesis chapter 1 through the third verse of chapter 2. Then, with an unmistakable preface ("These are the generations of the heavens and the earth when they were created") begins a second, radically different from the first both in large aspects (no day-by-day creation with a rest on the seventh day) and in small details (birds come out of the water in the first story, Genesis 1:20, but are made out of the earth in the second, Genesis 2:19). A little later comes the tale of Noah and the Flood. How many of each kind of animal did Noah take into the Ark? Most people would instantly answer: "Two." That is what God tells Noah to do in Genesis 6:19–20, and that is what Noah does in Genesis 7:15–16: logically he takes pairs, one male and one female. Yet in Genesis 7:2–3 God explicitly orders Noah to take in birds and clean animals *by sevens* and unclean animals *by twos*. Noah does nothing about this, and the command is expressly contradicted in the same chapter (Genesis 7:9: "two and two, . . . as God had commanded Noah"). God cannot have given two different and conflicting commands; Noah cannot have chosen which command he should obey. Obviously the curious distinction between clean animals by sevens and unclean animals by twos was simply inserted into the text by someone who wanted to imply that the rules for kosher food went far back, even before the Flood. The stories of Creation and the story of the Flood: they have been read and reread for many generations; but how many readers have ever noticed these discrepancies or tried to account for them?

The longer and more impressive a book is, the larger and more complex a subject is, the more difficult most people find it to see the overall structure with all its articulations. This the prudent teacher will remember. He will teach his own subject, whatever it may be, not as a gravelly conglomerate of facts and details and techniques, but as a single intellectual construct, which his pupils will gradually come to perceive as a whole. Each course he teaches must be planned with that principle in mind. At the outset the students should be given an outline showing the field which they are going to cover. Usually they will not read it. Being still short-sighted and immature, they instinctively shrink from large-scale systems. Knowing this, the teacher will go over the outline with them, explaining how the individual parts mesh together and ultimately form a total pattern. This is why Wittgenstein in his latter days was such a tantalizing and disappointing teacher of philosophy. He planned nothing. He wrote nothing down, or very little, but brooded all the time over problems of thought and language—except during those short respites when he sat in the front row and drank in his favorite opiate, a large, silly, brightly colored motion picture.* Therefore, each time his pupils assembled, he did not embark on a planned intellectual voyage on which they could accompany him. He simply started putting into words the current phase of his long-continued dialogue with himself. Occasionally he would become aware that he was talking to them about something he had not thought over and coaxed or bullied into shape. Having no scheme, he would stop short, and sit in tightly clenched silence, or else break out into self-reproach: "You have a very stupid

---

*N. Malcolm with G.H. von Wright, *Ludwig Wittgenstein* (New York, 1958).

teacher today!" Awed but baffled, his pupils were reduced to writing down his aphorisms and assembling them as well as they could into something resembling trains of thought. The transcripts, published as *The Blue and Brown Books* (New York, 1958), are perplexing to read, for they contain many abrupt statements which, if uttered in dialogue, would surely have provoked searching questions and criticisms. Such was the force of Wittgenstein's personality that they were accepted and recorded and treasured—as the followers of Pythagoras sanctified that philosopher's authoritative statements with the phrase: "He Himself said it."

Still, Wittgenstein *was* teaching, teaching a special attitude to a special subject. He was inculcating into his pupils a grand negation. Truth, he felt, can never be completely attained, or adequately expressed in words; and philosophy is an endless search, a Faustian pilgrimage. Teachers of other subjects cannot and should not try to imitate his thinking or his manner, else they will discourage their students, and eventually themselves.

As well as the overall scheme of the course, so laid out that both teacher and pupils always know where they are and where they are making for, the college teacher should prepare each meeting of the class, determining, within the time allotted, to raise a certain number of questions and answer them or evoke answers to them; to communicate an interlocking series of facts and demonstrate their connections; to explain one particular aspect of a historical process. After a session, the students ought to feel that they have started from one point, traversed intervening areas and surmounted obstacles, and reached a satisfactory halting place. One of the most disheartening intellectual experiences I ever underwent was to hear Plato's *Republic* discussed by a philosopher who simply sat down with the text in his hand and chatted about it. *The Republic* is a magnificently organized work, in eleven parts each with its own character, and with a larger and more complex structure underlying this clear division. It opens quietly, with a chance meeting of friends, and Socrates talking with an aged man; it closes superbly, with a vast vision of the life after death. Often, in its grandeur and control, it reminds me of a Beethoven symphony. But of this we learned little or nothing from the amiable and even condescendingly light conversation of our teacher. No doubt we learned much by finding it out for ourselves; but some of us never fully realized it. When Plato composed *The Republic* he designed it as carefully as Ictinus planned the Parthenon. To ignore or minimize this architectonic quality is to do a grave injustice to a great writer, and to obscure one of the finest achievements of the Greek genius, its capacity for strong yet subtle structure.

By insisting that planning is essential, I do not mean that each class, or the entire course, should be mechanically regulated, with no room for spontaneous questions, unrehearsed arguments, and ad libs. Many of the best moments in teaching appear out of nowhere and must be seized before they vanish. A segment of a lesson, a few paragraphs of a lecture, can well be sacrificed for the sake of a new and striking idea—provided always that the general scheme is clear in everyone's mind. In a concerto there often comes a moment when the orchestra stops playing, while the soloist displays his dexterity and taste in a long flourish which appears to be improvised, and in the eighteenth and nineteenth centuries sometimes was. He sounds as though he had taken off in flight and was soaring above the solid ground of the concerto, swooping and whirling like a skydiver, until at last, triumphantly, he lands upon a waiting orchestral chord. A good teacher should aim at doing this now and again, catching a fresh idea as it emerges and improvising on it —giving both himself and his pupils the delight of the unexpected, and then (before too long) returning to the central theme of his discourse.

Before he gives the first lecture, the college teacher will have done one of the most disagreeable and most necessary parts of his work. He will have a bibliography ready for distribution. He will have confirmed that the textbooks really exist, in sufficient numbers, and that they are easy to obtain. He will have prepared a list of topics for his students—in term papers or experiments or field-work—to investigate.

But before he gives his first lecture on the same subject next year, he will have changed his notes, striking out some sections and adding others. Naturally. Inevitably. He himself will have modified some of his earlier ideas. A new book on the subject will have been published. Special studies will have appeared in periodicals. If they are controversial, he must grapple with them; if they contain new information, he must digest it and tell his students about it. My colleague Moses Hadas told me, looking back on it with incredulous horror, that he had once attended the classes of a senior professor who *read* the same lectures aloud every year (though surely he knew them well enough to deliver them by rote) with such systematic monotony that he stopped, at the end of each session, exactly where, ten years or twenty years earlier, he had put a tick in the margin. Such a man is unworthy of the names of scholar and teacher. He can never even have glanced at the annual bibliographies covering his own subject. In the field which I know best, *L'Année Philologique* reports the publication of new books and summarizes new articles on classical philology. These articles are drawn from something like five hundred periodicals in many languages; and the entire bibliographical apparatus for one year fills over 750 pages, together with copious indexes.* Similar collections appear every year or oftener in most important areas of scholarship. It is a positive duty for every college teacher to go through the sections covering the topics in which he himself is working, to follow up every lead he discovers, and to incorporate the results in his annually revised lectures.

As he reads each book or article, he should summarize it—not on those evasive little 3″ × 5″ cards, but on quarto sheets to be placed in a loose-leaf book or a file folder— noting its authorship, date and place of publication, length by pages; and finally adding the date he read it and the general impression it made upon him. Important sentences, useful data, crucial references, should be copied out verbatim, as well as the names of other works cited by the author, on which further investigation might be valuable. Such a summary is the next best thing to having one's own copy of the book; and books are often hard to obtain. Among my files I have summaries of books (inaccessible here) which I read in Athens,

---

*This invaluable reference work does not summarize books, but lists the most important reviews of each book; it does summarize all articles, thus saving its readers much precious time by showing them what is and what is not within their competence.

Vienna, Milan, and Paris; books in the United States which exist in only one or two copies and which were procured for me through Inter-Library Loan; books which were once on the shelves at Columbia but have now been lost or mutilated or stolen; books which concerned me long ago but which I have now all but forgotten. Even to go through the files on a single subject never fails to stimulate my mind.

Often an aspiring college teacher is so devoted to his own subject that he never thinks of questioning its value. Yet that value may not be so evident to his pupils. Therefore he ought to examine his own purpose in studying and teaching it. Usually he will discover that he has several distinct aims in mind. For instance, if he is discussing the French Revolution, he can treat it as a vastly important episode in the history of Europe; as an upheaval which in various ways affected the young United States; as a catalyst for independence movements in Central and South America; as a case study in one of several patterns of development followed by revolutionary movements; as displaying the heroism and baseness, genius and stupidity, of individuals as well as the larger, slower movements of classes and masses; and as a continuing force in the mind of the French people. There are still royalists who support the claimant to the throne of the Bourbons and show their contempt for the Republic by putting the stamp with its effigy *("la grosse Marianne")* upside down on their letters; and, among the rebellious French students of 1968, some upheld Jacobin ideals and others deliberately recalled the *Enragés*, the anarchists of the Revolution. The teacher should be clear in his own mind about these different approaches to the subject, each valuable in a different way: he should know to which he gives priority; and at some time—whether at the opening of the course, or in a final summary, or by stages as he proceeds—he will explain them to the students. Behind the facts, which heaven knows are confusing and elusive enough, loom the larger forces of history: these are the teacher's true concern.

Communication is the young teacher's most perplexing problem. And before discussing it we must face the painful fact that the teacher does not always create the difficulty. Some types of pupil are averse to learning anything whatever; and some resist being instructed by teachers whose race or color or social origin or religion or politics they distrust and dislike. This is common, alas, in American schools: less common in American colleges and universities, yet there too it has always existed. Mark Hopkins, the ideal of American teachers, experienced that aversion. He said that if there was no enthusiasm for learning in a class, only the teacher can understand "the anxiety, I had almost said agony, with which, as the prophet of old on the dead body of the child, he once and again as it were puts his mouth to its mouth, and his eyes to its eyes, and stretches himself upon the class, and feels no life come.* And he alone knows how cheerless and hopeless and slavish is the dull routine of his labors after that. There are, it seems to me, few modes of gaining a living, short of actual villainy,

---

*This metaphor, which sounds unintentionally comic today, was very serious in an age when people read their Bible. Hopkins was recalling the miracle by which Elijah restored a dying boy to life: 1 Kings 17:17-24.

which a man of sensibility would not prefer to it!"*
Hostility between students and teachers has been growing, both in the United States and abroad, during recent
years. I have seldom experienced it myself, and I regret
that I can suggest no remedy for it, except the preserva-
tion (difficult enough at all times, and harder now) of
calmness, decency, and impartiality.

When the pupils wish to learn, the teacher must put
no obstacles in their way—including himself. First of all,
he must be clear. THOU SHALT NOT (he will tell himself)
yield to bad habits of—er—speech; talk in a weak or
wavering or slovenly voice; utter incoherent sentences to
baffle the listeners; use abstruse words *(parameter, rapport, chiliastic, Weltanschauung, reductionist)* without explanation; introduce unfamiliar proper names ("as Condor-
cet says") without spelling them or writing them out;†
throw off untranslated quotations in foreign languages
("Schiller puts it extremely well, *'mit der Dummheit
kämpfen Götter selbst vergebens'* "). Not long ago a young
officer in the U.S. Marine Corps faced his first command.
As a platoon-leader, he had to make emotional and intellectual contact with his men, so that they would obey
and follow him. In the first three minutes, he partly won
them over through addressing each by his name and his
town of origin. Then he lost them forever—by telling
them a funny story which lasted five minutes and had the
punch line in French.

(That particular affectation was common during the

---

*Leverett Wilson Spring, *Mark Hopkins, Teacher* (New York, 1888),
pp. 115–116.

†A high school student recently wrote, in a paper on Eugene
O'Neill, that for one of his dramas he was given the Pullet Surprise.

last century, and in the most unexpected places. For instance, Conan Doyle originally conceived Sherlock Holmes as a purely scientific thinker, devoted to chemistry, anatomy, and practical geology. "Knowledge of literature—nil," says Dr. Watson in the second chapter of *A Study in Scarlet*, summing up his curious new roommate. But by the end of the sixth chapter in *The Sign of Four* we find Holmes citing Goethe's *Faust* [*Wir sind gewohnt, dass die Menschen verhöhnen/Was sie nicht verstehn:* Part 1, Scene 3] and adding the comment "Goethe is always pithy." I cannot think of a less appropriate way to describe the style of Goethe: perhaps Doyle simply took the quotation from a reference book, wrote it down, and then said to himself: "Goethe is always . . . hm, what shall we say? Goe*the*, pi*thy*, that's it." The same tale closes with Holmes applying to himself a quotation from the *Xenien*, a set of satirical epigrams by Goethe and Schiller which can hardly have been the bedside reading of any busy consulting detective. A little later, at the end of *The Red-Headed League*, Holmes describes his own vocation in a French phrase borrowed from a letter of Gustave Flaubert; while *A Case of Identity* is rounded off with an epigram from Hafiz—fortunately not in the original Persian. Doyle was imitating his model Poe, who also loved to display his erudition even in snippets. *The Murders in the Rue Morgue* ends with a citation from Rousseau, who would scarcely have appealed to the intellectual Auguste Dupin of the 1830s; while *The Purloined Letter* [1845] has Dupin sending his outwitted rival a line from the forgotten baroque tragedian Crébillon [*Atrée*, 1707]—a line painfully lacking in point, except that it is in the language of superior culture.)

Next in importance is vitality, energy, drive. The

young are easily bored, often sleepy, sometimes nowadays drug- or drink-dizzy. If their teacher is half dead, or stiff and mechanical in manner, or cocooned within a thick protective covering, they will learn less than they could, less than they should. A British peer was once making a speech in the House of Lords. In the middle of it he broke off, and yawned. Lord Ellenborough, the presiding officer, remarked: "Come, come, the fellow shows some symptoms of good taste; but he is trespassing on our prerogative." The young will be less charitable than that, and less witty. Therefore it is fatal to go on throughout the hour and throughout the whole course at the same pace. Every change of tone enlivens interest. Each variation of tempo and emphasis inspirits not only the student but the teacher.

In all but the most advanced classes, timing matters. Teachers love talking. Students do not enjoy being passive recipients of talk: at least for more than the stipulated period. Therefore, watch the clock: never overrun your time. If you do, you are either depriving them of a little leisure (perhaps even a meal) or cutting into some colleague's allotment of precious minutes. Sometimes a class will urge its teacher to go on, and will ignore the bell signaling the end of the period. Sometimes. It is a compliment. It is not frequently bestowed. If it is not, then produce a few memorable final words; and stop.

Of all these efforts, the aim is communication, or rather communion: sharing the experience of learning and understanding. The teacher will not talk *at* the class. He will talk *with* it. There are certain philosophical themes, says Plato, on which he has never written and never will write a book. They cannot be expressed, like other types of learning, in words; but after long communion between teacher and student, suddenly, as it were, a spark leaps out of the fire and kindles the student's soul and burns there independently.*

As for guidance and discipline, their secrets will be learned by every successful teacher from his own experience. But a few of them can be pointed out to novices.

It is necessary always to dominate a class. The teacher need not be a martinet, but he must control behavior, reprove inattention, and guide the movement of thought —keeping discussions from straying into vagueness, preventing laggards from sitting back and daydreaming (by prodding them with unexpected questions), welding each class into a group which he re-creates at each meeting. Variety of pace and tone will prevent the students from dropping into a comfortable somnolent jogtrot. Humor is invaluable, to restrain the extravagant and to spur on the dullards.

Relaxation is helpful. Three or four minutes of every hour can well be given to lighter discourse—comments on a new book, notes on something read in that day's paper (something relevant, not the signal for a political Donnybrook Fair). When the students' minds are switched on once more, they will be livelier and more receptive.

Examinations, tests, term papers should be treated with scrupulous care, particularly by beginning teachers, since the students often suspect them of being ignorant, biased, or hypocritical. All such material must be read with intimate attention and every possible means of ensuring impartiality. It should also be scrutinized with

---

*Plato, *Letters* 7. 341c4–d2.

a wary and suspicious eye. A student who is tongue-tied in class may sometimes express himself with surprising fluency in a written paper; but he or she may have copied those fluent paragraphs and those well-chosen quotations from a couple of books found in the library; or even bought the whole thing ready-made from a term-paper factory. I once received a long essay turned in by an intelligent and industrious young man. Hand-written, packed with tight arguments and apt citations, it looked like a good deal of hard work. The only odd thing was that the style changed in pace and quality about one-third of the way through: as though he had written the first part of it, and then waited some weeks before going on to the second. Or else—but I could not see this man as commanding two different prose styles and using them on the same topic. Or as if he had copied some of it from an external source. An afternoon in the library gave me the solution. He had copied all of it verbatim from *two* sources, and had made no effort to rewrite his models in such a way as to cover up the join or diminish the dissimilarity of style. He had reproduced them so faithfully and so unintelligently that he had transcribed three of their misprints; but not too faithfully either, for at one point (the turnover of a page) he had dropped out three lines, and gone doggedly on, fitting the head of one sentence to the tail of another.

Every student's written work should be read with attention, with sympathy, and with suspicion. First and foremost, with attention. Comments added by the examiner must be clear and comprehensible: it is worse than useless, it is irritating for the writer of an essay to see its margin studded with hasty and inadequate notes such as "X," "??," and "awk." When anything is marked wrong, the correct solution should always be given: or at least an indication where it will be found.

Some teachers find it helpful, even after the examination is over and the results have been posted, to digest their verdict upon it and upon the whole term's work into a page or two—pointing out errors frequently committed, warning against underlying misconceptions, and praising specially felicitous work—and to circulate this as a farewell letter to the class. Its tone (even if it mentions mistakes) should be encouraging and congratulatory.

These are the main techniques of teaching which the newly graduated college teacher ought to know. But when is he or she to learn them, and from whom?

In a special course on teacher-training, to be taken while he or she is doing graduate work and writing the dissertation? No. The doctoral degree is a valuable one. It cannot be earned without mastering a wide range of skills and subjects: it occupies nearly all the candidate's time. To add a course on educational techniques to it would either overburden the graduands or dilute their work. Some years ago the New York Academy of Medicine discussed how and when medical students should be taught the history of their science. Senior physicians said they were often appalled to see how little was known by their young successors either about great discoveries such as the circulation of the blood or about great men such as Osler and Cushing. Yet they concluded that it was utterly impracticable to make room for a course in the subject at any stage of medical training; and that it fell to individual lecturers, each dealing with his special field, to introduce a few essential facts and some stimulating remarks about its historical development.

In the same way it is the duty of an adviser as he steers each student through the doctoral examinations, and a sponsor as he supervises the writing of the thesis, to remember that he is training not only a research scholar but a teacher; to give him hints on method and warnings against mistakes; to throw in illustrative reminiscences dealing with his own career; to tell him about good teachers whom he has known either personally or through his reading; and to recommend articles and books which evoke their work and personality. R.W. Clark's history of the Huxley family (New York, 1968) would delight and stimulate any aspiring scientist. In the library I often browse through the stately volumes of the *Proceedings of the British Academy*: each of which ends with detailed and sympathetic memoirs of those members of the Academy who have died during the preceding year. These are men of recognized achievement, but the difficulties they had to face are not understressed. To read of their succeeding, against many obstacles, warms the blood.

A future college teacher will do well to watch many of his own profession at work. He should attend lectures even on subjects outside his own field, if he hears that the lecturer is effective; and get permission to sit in on a few seminars directed by eminent men and women. He should seize the opportunity of hearing distinguished visitors. If they are good, he will gain much from each experience; if they are bad, he will learn what to avoid. At the age of nineteen, although keen on Greek and Latin, I nearly dropped the subjects altogether. A scholar visiting Glasgow University from Cambridge gave a lecture which we were all encouraged to attend.

It was entitled *Scripta Minoa*. In my second year of university work, I understood neither the title nor the topic; and the whole thing was not *spoken to us*, but read out from typescript in a high fruity voice which struck the sturdy Scots as ludicrously affected. My friends and I were so puzzled, so baffled and discouraged, that we walked home wondering whether we should change to a different and more intelligible field of study. Yet the subject of the lecture—when later I came to understand it—was a good one: the decipherment of one of the mysterious scripts found on clay tablets in Crete. The visiting scholar's solution to the mystery turned out to be wrong.* Listening to her, we could not tell whether it was wrong or right; but that need not have mattered. What she could have done, but did not attempt to do, was to explain the various methods of deciphering cryptographic writing in an unknown language, and thus, while leading us on to the conclusion she favored, whet our intellects to attempt something of the kind ourselves. Michael Ventris, who did the final decipherment, was not by profession a classicist. He was an architect. His

---

*It was finally solved by Michael Ventris in 1952: see J. Chadwick, *The Decipherment of Linear B* (Cambridge, 1967²). Her solution was published in 1931, not by her own university press, but by a London firm, as *A Clue to the Cretan Scripts*. Essentially it is an attempt to interpret the shapes of the Cretan signs by comparing them with the shapes of Egyptian hieroglyphs and Phoenician consonant symbols, which is not too far-fetched. But some of her results were dismally unconvincing: for example, one little inscription was transcribed as "*Koo, ko, ko, ko, ko, Ne, ko,*" meaning, "Listen, list, list, list, list, Mother of Waters, list!" All the same, she was right in the basic idea, that the scripts—or at least one of them—represented an early stage of the language we know as Greek: the idea which even Ventris resisted for a long time.

interest in the problem began when, as a schoolboy of fourteen, he heard a talk by the explorer and re-creator of ancient Crete, Sir Arthur Evans, which pointed to the mystery of the still unread Cretan scripts. He vowed to solve it; and he did. As for me, in time I recovered from the numbing effect of that terrible lecture and continued studying the classics; but it stayed with me as a lesson on what to avoid, yea, by Allah (as they say in *The Arabian Nights*), were it graven with a needle upon the eye corners, it were a warning to whoso would be warned.

Furthermore, in some fields, though not in all, a graduate student can find time and opportunity to teach one or two elementary classes, and thus gain a little preliminary experience. His adviser and the chief of his department should keep a watchful eye on him or her at this time, and feel no compunction at explaining how the classes should be handled.

After graduation. This is the hardest time for all young scholars, starting to teach, striving to continue research and publish some of their work, coping with poverty and insecurity, sometimes beset by family problems, and numbingly aware (unless they are both gifted and lucky) that they face an uphill climb which will last not years, but decades. Now is the period when they most need encouragement. It is for their senior colleagues to give them help, to listen to them discussing their difficulties, and to keep a watchful eye on their work as teachers. Often an unpromising youth or inhibited girl will, after the triumph of winning the degree, expand into energy and versatility unexpected even to themselves. They need only a little control. Often the effort of completing the dissertation exhausts the young graduate, and when confronted with teaching primary classes on a far lower level, he collapses into resentful ennui. He or she must be given reassurance and cheer.

In some American colleges the dean will furnish additional guidance to teachers starting their careers. Students report on all or most of their courses and instructors. The dean's advisers consolidate these reports, and as a result are often able to tell a young teacher that he is bad at this or good at that: he is exciting to listen to, but atrociously unpunctual, sometimes missing a session without apology; he is very knowledgeable, but cannot be heard beyond the first four rows of the lecture room; he devotes all his attention to four or five bright students and ignores the rest; and so forth.

Ultimately the responsibility rests on the college teacher himself. He must be constantly aware that it is necessary to keep his teaching vital, and to renew it year by year as the subject develops and he himself changes. He must never feel embarrassed about asking for advice and assistance. And he must never relax his attention to his work, remembering that, just as an ignorant or negligent physician can spoil a human body, so a careless or thoughtless teacher can spoil a young mind.

COMMUNICATION

Nowadays, when you talk to young men and women of
college age, they do not hear you very well. Their
thoughts are elsewhere. They say: "Right," and they say:
"What was that again?" But their eyes do not quite focus.
Nor do their minds.

We cannot blame them. The best we can do is to sym-
pathize, to try to keep them calm, and to recall what it
was like for us ourselves to be young, and to be faced
with unemployment (1929–), war (1941–), cold war (1948–),
war (1950–), racial conflict (1954–), war (1963–), and the
other crises which have been chronic ailments of the
twentieth century. Still, it makes it much more difficult
to teach them.

Have you ever attempted to take a long-distance call
in the middle of a party at someone else's house? The
host says: "This is for you, Cleveland calling," and hands
you the receiver. Distant and uneven, a little voice speaks
in your ear, explaining something you have forgotten

and asking questions you cannot answer. From time to time it is interrupted by surges and crackles of electricity; occasionally the voice of a total stranger, like a disembodied ghost, floats along the wire uttering fragments of an unintelligible conversation. But your caller in Cleveland goes on earnestly explaining and eagerly enquiring. Meanwhile your host has gone back to the other guests, and is engaged in a loud argument about the Middle East that comes into your free ear with much more force and stridency than the Cleveland talker. Two late-comers are taking off their coats and chatting just beside you in the hall. Music is coming from the middle distance, where Jeff and Valerie have been persuaded to do their own special version of "Baby, it's cold outside"; and there are shouts of laughter at the end of each verse. And you are hemmed in by a stream of miscellaneous noise, random interjections and isolated phrases and hum and clink and clatter, topped off by the furious blares of taxis threading their way past the double-parked cars outside the door. At last Cleveland says: "O.K., you've got all that. Nine o'clock on Tuesday without fail, and bring *both* zizms, they're sending Presjunks as well. 'Bye now." And you go back to the party, wondering what on earth that was all about, and trying with a sense of overhanging despair to make a connected story out of the message. Sometimes you ring back next morning for confirmation. Sometimes you put the bits together into the wrong shape, and blame the telephone company. Sometimes you get it right, and it is at least partly luck.

Anyone who teaches young men and young women today is in the situation of the man calling from Cleveland. He has a consistent and carefully prepared message to deliver. They know something of what he is trying to tell them, and they have one ear open for his message.

They will listen. But their attention is distracted, not intermittently but continuously, by a torrent of other voices and excitements through which his communication can only with difficulty make its way.

To begin with, they are young. And youth, with its health and energy, is (despite all the dangers that beset it) rather like being at a perpetual party. We oldsters (they think) lead shockingly dull lives. Certainly we have far fewer pleasures. We could scarcely endure their enjoyments and excitements even if we tried. Recently I reread some of the diaries I kept when I was at college, and they made me dizzy. Into one week I tried to cram as much activity as would now keep me hopping for a month or more: a debate in which I spoke, a boxing lesson in which I became speechless, a meeting of the musical society to arrange the next term's concerts, an angry session of the magazine board, correspondence with a French author one of whose plays I was translating, special preparation for a highly competitive scholarship exam—not to mention the regular three hours of lectures plus writing one essay and one piece of Latin verse and one piece of Greek prose and doing a sizable amount of peripheral reading "recommended though not prescribed." No wonder that, when I look through my old lecture notes, I sometimes see a page where my pen faltered and grew enfeebled and finally trailed away into a downward curve

as the warm, airless lecture hall and the monotonous voice of the lecturer and the many missed hours of sleep enfolded me in a soporific embrace. All these things were occupying my mind at the same time.

Exciting, yes, and the essence of growth; but distracting. To sit and listen to a systematic exposition of vector analysis or the policy of the U.S.S.R. toward non-Russian ethnic groups, difficult enough for an adult, is tormentingly arduous for a young man or woman. Sometimes in the classroom I look at them with real astonishment, wondering what on earth keeps them in their seats when every one of them is a mass of explosive forces ready to enter the critical state.

The biggest excitement of all, the one which corresponds to the cocktails at the party, is love. Usually their minds are at least half occupied by love for at least half of the time. Either they are in love—and are puzzled by its power, or saddened by its cruelties, or terrified by its dangers, or exultant in its delights; or else they are lonely and would like to be loved, but cannot find anyone lovable or loving; or else they know and practice sexual intercourse but find it repetitive and either degrading or at least inadequate to bring together and satisfy all the longings which they feel active in their minds and bodies, because a single note is not a harmony. For a teacher it is strange to look at those young faces, and to reflect that although their owners are mentally immature, physically they are adults, and may well have children of their own. That quiet little character in the front seat, with the thick pebble glasses, seems to be concentrating hard on the methods of establishing the Gross National Product, but he is also trying to decide whether, since he is too unattractive ever to catch a real beauty, he ought to abandon the idea of love altogether and become a recluse: a hermit of the intelligence. Farther back, the calm girl with the dainty ponytail is taking down the figures with apparent interest and efficiency, but she is also wondering whether she is going to have a baby, for she married another graduate student last year, and they agreed to postpone the family until they both had their degrees, and yet. . . .

Older people—I almost wrote "grown-ups," but these youngsters are grown up in many ways—older people have usually had enough experience and have thought enough about love to know what it can do to them and how they should live with it. For the young it is all new. Sometimes I think there are only four sovereign experiences in life: the baby's discovery of the world outside itself, the youth's and girl's discovery of love, and the adult's discovery of art and of religion. All of these are overwhelming in their excitement. They transform the personality. But the difficulty about the discovery of love is that it competes, with almost irresistible power (don't I remember?), against the training of the intellect; and yet both must go on at the same time.

Then there are other distractions which, like the music pouring out of the party, keep the message from being fully heard or even fully attended to. Instead of listening to your man in Cleveland, you would rather be inside listening to Jeff and Valerie singing. In the same way young men and women can scarcely ever concentrate 100 percent, or even 80 percent, on the intellectual messages which their teachers send them: because their will power is not yet fully trained. Very few students ever go through a course without wondering at least twice or thrice whether they ought not to drop it. Very few ever complete their education without having several periods of discouragement, almost amounting to despair, when they almost decide it would be better to throw up the whole thing, and either take a job or push off to wander round the world. If there is a good job handy it is all the more difficult to resist such a temptation. One of my friends, who is now a successful surgeon, used to play with me in the college dance band: sax and clarinet. He was good. We were all, as a combo, pretty good; but he was special. People came to hear him. Suddenly out of the blue he was offered the equivalent of $300 a week to turn professional. Although he had entered college in order to become a physician, although he had made his way by scholarships and had been passing all his examinations, although he really liked the profession and had already mapped out future lines of research for himself, he still had a long period of doubt, when that $300 a week, so close, so easy, and "This is only the start," looked far more attractive than the long years of training and internship before a distant and uphill career. He used to talk to me about it for hours, when he should have been studying the ductless glands; and I used to discuss its pros and cons by the hour, when I should have been reading Lucan on the civil wars of Rome.

Another distraction, new in these last two decades, is provided by drugs. Some young men used to drink hard and smash up their cars. Now they use hard drugs and smash up both their bodies and their minds. Some years ago, when all this was new, an undergraduate living in one of the dormitories at Columbia OD'd (= died of an overdose of heroin). One of the senior men on the faculty somberly told me that this was a turning point in the history of American universities: a crisis after which things would never be the same, and were likely to grow worse rather than better. No doubt there is an important distinction between the user of soft drugs and the user of hard drugs, just as there is a difference between the social drinker and the lush; yet it is always possible, and even tempting, for one to change into the other; and in youth it is hard and distracting to resist temptation.

There is not much that a teacher *as a teacher* can do about this problem—except, obviously, by setting an example: that is, by being himself well-balanced and energetic and orderly and healthy and not dependent on artificial stimuli. But he must look out for the symptoms of drug addiction, in order to warn his colleagues, to inform the appropriate disciplinary authorities, and when necessary to communicate with the parents. Simple manifestations such as drowsiness and inattention may be the result of a roistering weekend, or even of some virtuous excess such as several late nights of study. There is, however, one important symptom to watch for —the symptom, or rather the injury, which young men and women never expect and cannot themselves diagnose. This is a serious change in personality.

Between the ages of eighteen and twenty-five no character is fully defined. The growing youth and girl are busy, every day and every hour, molding an amorphous amalgam of instincts and inherited traits and familial behavior patterns and desires and ambitions and physical urges into some kind of cohesive shape. The chief danger of drugs is that they break up the mold. They dissolve the character which was gradually with effort becoming something solid. They shape it into a new form, far less stable, far less healthy, far less happy. The worst of it is that the victim usually does not realize he is changing, far less that the change is likely to be irre-

versible until it ends in chaos and destruction. All teachers who are reasonably alert will see the personalities of
their pupils changing—usually, it is to be hoped, for the
better. But now in a drug-infected culture they must
look out for signs of deterioration. A photographer who
develops his own films finds it a ticklish but rewarding
job. In the darkroom, under the dim red light, he passes
the film through the liquid. At first blank and gray, it
begins to show shapes and tints, the foreground stands
out while the background builds itself up, and the whole
composition he saw in the viewfinder or the reflex as he
pressed the button now begins to reappear. At this moment, should one drop of acid fall into the solution, the
picture blurs, warps, writhes into a hideous freak. Just
as drastically as this can a young drug-taker become a
monster; but not so rapidly. The deformation can sometimes be arrested and even turned back, if its first symptoms are observed in good time. It is now, alas, the duty
of a teacher to watch his pupils for signs of changing and
deteriorating personality.

   War (said the historian Thucydides) is a violent
teacher. And it is extremely hard for any human teacher
to compete with war for the attention of his students.
They can scarcely concentrate on long preparation and
careful thinking (which are the essence of a sound education) if a violent interruption may alter their entire lives.
The whole problem of war has recently become far more
complicated, far more difficult to discuss rationally.
Since the surrender of Germany and Japan put a satisfactory end to the last worldwide conflict, the minds of our
students have gone through three different phases. At
first they all felt the horrible threat of a confrontation

between Russia and the United States in which atomic weapons might be used. An intelligent and sensitive girl told me in 1950 that sometimes, when she crossed over from her classroom to the big library, the buildings around her seemed to quiver and their outlines to grow vague as though they might at any moment dissolve and, "like an insubstantial pageant faded, leave not a rack behind." One of her classmates was haunted by a forgotten poem written long ago by an obscure poet, as though it were a premonition of the last days of humanity.

> When the world is burning,
> Fired within, yet turning
>   Round with face unscathed;
> Ere fierce flames, uprushing,
> O'er all lands leap, crushing,
>   Till earth fall, fire-swathed;
> Up amidst the meadows,
> Gently through the shadows,
>   Gentle flames will glide,
> Small, and blue, and golden. . . .
>
> Where the dance is sweeping,
> Through the greensward peeping,
>   Shall the soft lights start;
> Laughing maids, unstaying,
> Deeming it trick-playing,
> High their robes upswaying,
>   O'er the lights shall dart;
> And the woodland haunter
> Shall not cease to saunter

> When, far down some glade,
> Of the great world's burning,
> One soft flame upturning
> Seems, to his discerning,
> Crocus in the shade.*

That terror very slowly receded into the back of the mind. Then came the Korean War. A clear case of unprovoked aggression, resisted by the United Nations, it seemed for a time to be a just war, almost a crusade. Yet, as it dragged on and on, it grew more confusing and more squalid: necessary, perhaps, but sickening. It was scarcely ended by an armistice before we found ourselves being sucked into another war, in Vietnam. It was this that really jolted many students (and many of their teachers) into states of emotional disturbance which continued and grew more and more disorderly and painful, month after month. They felt the war to be in the highest degree unnecessary; miserably wasteful of money and lives; stupidly run, both from a diplomatic and from a military point of view; immoral; a massive crime. They found it almost impossible to concentrate. They were distracted, like a rat in a maze with no center and no exit and the floor and walls gradually heating into a red glow. Many of them felt that all normal study was useless, since the world, or at least their part of it, had gone mad. Drug use increased rapidly; so did purposeless rudeness and violence and mob action.

I still remember, as vividly as a nightmare, a doctoral examination which came up at the end of a peculiarly

---

*This is by Ebenezer Jones (1820–1860), "the neglected poet" who was admired by Browning and Rossetti, but had no success and abandoned the art.

painful academic year. The candidate was a shy and nervous young man: his work was good enough, but he was inhibited in discussing it. The examination was held in a small room without air-conditioning. Since it was an important and confidential function we had to keep the door closed. If we kept the windows shut, the temperature rose and the oxygen supply in the air dwindled and the fumes of my neighbor's pipe grew intolerable. If we opened the windows, the inflamed oratory of a speaker leading a protest rally rushed in, magnified by a bullhorn and punctuated by rhythmic shouts of applause which hideously reminded me of the SIEG HEIL SIEG HEIL SIEG HEIL of a Hitler demonstration—so that both the gentle questions of the examiners and the timid replies of the candidate were drowned. If we adjourned to another room, we feared he might break down; if we adjourned to another time, well, he might never get going again. Meanwhile there were obscure noises of scuffling and bumping just outside the door, which we did our best to ignore. At last—perhaps because he saw that we all sympathized with him and were all suffering too—the candidate brightened up and took fire and delivered a fine five-minute explanation of a central point in his work. The chairman sighed with relief. The sponsor, nodding with approval, sat back in his chair. At that moment the door burst open. A barefooted girl with dirty straggling hair walked in, said: "The building's occupied," and walked out again just in time to miss the door, which the sponsor slammed behind her scarred and filthy heels. But now, with a fresh supply of adrenalin gushing into his bloodstream, the candidate continued to talk lucidly and cogently. Twenty minutes later the examination was declared satisfactorily concluded, his dissertation was accepted "subject to minor revisions *(discuss them with your sponsor and get notes from each examiner),"* and his career was, in spite of several unforeseeable difficulties, assured. His only remaining problem, like ours, was how to get out of the building, with furniture piled ten feet high in the entrance lobby and the dirty girl sitting on top of it picking her scabs.

That was a bad time for teachers and learners. At least that particular war is over; some of the tension has been released; once again we can communicate with students. We can help to train their will power and shape their minds. What the young learn in college is not primarily sets of facts, or special skills, or theories. They learn how to think. This is the most important development of all, for it changes them into capable adults. Some of them never learn it properly. Uneducated people all over the world seldom learn it. That is why there is such a terrifying gulf between those who can think logically in general terms, and those who cannot. Those who think are able to see the world as a complex of events and forces which can be understood by fitting them into a number of intellectual patterns. History is one such pattern; economics is trying to become another; philosophy used to be one, but has grown arid and unhelpful. But those who have never learned logical thinking can rarely see these patterns. Generally they refuse to believe that the patterns exist, or that they are important. They substitute vague emotional burps for logic. Or else—when anyone tries to explain a pattern to them—they believe the explanation is "only a lot of talk," words, words, words, intended not to communicate but to deceive. Most authors who have written about the peasants of Russia agree in saying that, though often shrewd at solving particular problems, the peasants would not accept logical arguments because they did not believe in the possibility of understanding things by logic. Winston Churchill, in his history of World War II, quotes Stalin himself as feeling this difficulty. "You explain a plan carefully to the peasant," said Stalin, "and he scratches his head and says he must talk it over with his wife or his herdsman. Then he comes back and rejects the whole thing." It was not, apparently, that the peasant really understood the plan and opposed it, on carefully reasoned grounds. It was simply that he distrusted it because it was an intellectual structure, and he could not cope with intellectual structures any more than he could pull down a tree with his bare hands.

We see this kind of thing whenever we travel into remote areas of the world. Talking to illiterate farmers or isolated villagers in the back country of India or Latin America, even after the language difficulty has been partly solved, we feel another difficulty, this one insoluble. It is that they do not think as we do. They cannot make a general statement. Instead, they will tell a story. (That is why all the great religions of the world begin not with philosophical systems but with marvelous myths.) They cannot argue to reach a broad conclusion by to-and-fro discussions. At best, they will make counterstatements, and then stop. Long afterward, when we have left the village and gone home, they will remember us, with photographic vividness but without the power to generalize: we smoked a pipe *with a silver band,* or had a square *machine that clicked.* In their own land they are cleverer than we, and will survive where we might die. But outside their own land they will be miserable, since they cannot assimilate their new experiences and fit them into large general patterns.

So when we teach the young we have to remember

that, for a good deal of the time, they are trying to think as we do and not quite succeeding. Our minds are trained to put two and two together. Their minds are not yet trained to put anything together except emotional experiences. Our minds can detect remote similarities and build up large systems of thought. Indeed, if we have been successfully educated and successfully self-educated, that is what we go on doing all our lives. But their minds cannot make those jumps and fill in those connections: not yet.

Almost automatically, we single out cause and effect, principle and application, ground and variation, rule and exception, pro and con, general and particular. But these very concepts are strange to the young. In my teens I remember puzzling literally for years over the meaning of "cause." What is a "cause"? How can we say that the murder of an Austrian archduke "caused" a war? And what "caused" the murder itself? Was it the bullet, or the impulse of the murderer Gavrilo Princip, or his accurate aim, or the coincidence of his meeting the archduke at close quarters, or Serbian nationalist feeling, or the structure of the Hapsburg empire, or . . . ? It may sound silly, and yet this kind of thing worried me terribly: for I was a schoolboy during the First World War, and like millions of other people I felt that the war had been a terrible mistake—so that, if its *cause* could only be discovered, such a mistake could be prevented from ever happening again. It was really a revelation to me later, when I was taught how to analyze the idea of causation, and learned that there were several different interpretations of the word "cause"—Aristotle distinguished four types of cause, four—and that the entire concept of cause and effect was a human convenience in selecting from the process of events a few separate aspects which were important for our own purposes.

Here is the same problem restated for medical students. "One of the most frequent purposes of scientific papers relates to finding the cause of some phenomenon or condition, but most medical scientists seem completely oblivious (or ignorant) of the fact that results usually come from many causes, not one. I doubt if I could exaggerate my feelings regarding the stupidity we show in so frequently assuming that one result is due to only one cause. We ought to use the word 'why' in the plural, and ask: 'Whys is this patient in coma?' not: 'Why is this patient in coma?' The next time you hear someone say anything that attributes a single cause for some event, ask yourself if he means the predisposing, the precipitating, or the perpetuating cause? And how many causes of each of these kinds are involved?"* Here again is a short statement of principle by a historian. "In analyzing [a historical phenomenon] one mistake should be avoided: that of believing that, when the major cause has been identified, no other factors are relevant."†

And so it is with the young. Again and again, in talking to them, we use words which to us seem perfectly clear and simple. We say: "Now, there is an analogy. . . ." or: "Suppose we look for a precedent." They gaze dutifully at us, and they sometimes write it down, but they are not always quite sure what an analogy is, or what function a precedent performs. Therefore the wise teacher will always remember that it is not only the subject matter of his teaching that is new and strange to

---

*A. Gregg, *For Future Doctors* (Chicago, 1957), 81.
†O. Murray in *Journal of Roman Studies* 59 (1969), 264.

the class: it is the actual method of his thinking. And this the young have to learn. Without acquiring the principles of general reasoning, they will never be able fully to understand the laws of their country or grasp the meaning of its history; they will never be fit to organize a business or to detect a fallacy, to arrange their own lives or to educate their children.

But it is difficult to learn how to think: we must be patient with them while they learn it. When they do and say silly things, it is not an unnatural outburst of vice or folly: it is an upsurge of disorganized emotion, the random gesture of the animal, the child, or the savage out of which they are evolving.

This is why teaching is such a demanding profession. Doctors make sick people well again. Lawyers reconcile people's differences. Clergymen make people better in spirit. Teachers make children and youngsters, half animal and half savage, into civilized human beings. That would not be possible, of course, unless they wanted to undergo the change. Every child, every youth and girl, at heart wants to grow to the fullest powers of which he or she is capable. The best teachers in the world cannot force this growth. All they can ever do is to help it and encourage it. Their best reward is to see, not a "product," but a free and independent human being who can think.

THE
CLASS OF '64

The Chinese have an enormously large vocabulary of curses. Many of them are crude and cruel; but others are delicate innuendos, so subtle that they do not expect us Western barbarians to comprehend them. One of these in particular is attractive though cynical, and highly appropriate to this occasion. It is in the form of a malevolent wish: "May you pass the rest of your life in interesting times!" The Chinese have usually preferred tranquillity to stress, and monotony to revolution: for them, to live in an era when powerful historical forces are colliding with one another is an acute form of suffering.

For the next fifty or a hundred years we shall all be living in extremely interesting times. To cope with them we shall require all our courage, all our optimism, all our intelligence. But if, instead of going forward with the inexorable current of history, we were to go backward into the past, what should we discover? Should we find that, at some earlier period, there was less danger, and more—I shall not say comfort, for that is a vague, weak word—but more serenity and security and promise of peaceful fulfilment? Let us look at other years, and imagine what it would be like to be starting a career then.

Suppose this were the class, not of 1964, but of 1864. Gazing around the world, what should we see?

War, war everywhere: actual and exhausting, or impending and ominous. In the United States, the Civil War has been dragging along for more than three long years. Both sides are embittered and nearly desperate. Grant has just lost 55,000 men in the Wilderness campaign. At Cold Harbor, just a week ago, he committed the same appalling tactical error that Lee made last year at Gettysburg, by mounting a direct frontal attack on a very strong position. Finally, when he ordered the attack to be renewed, his men simply refused to move. Grant has failed. And the South is still full of fight. Next month Jubal Early will lead a sortie of seasoned Southern troops against the capital city of Washington, though he will not take it. In Europe two great disturbers of the peace are active. The chief threat is considered to be Napoleon the Third of France: brilliant and unprincipled, he has kept Europe in turmoil for ten years, and has just invaded the American continent, landing a French expeditionary force to set up a European prince as emperor of Mexico. But in Prussia Bismarck is just emerging as a plotter far more brilliant and even more dangerous. He has contrived to arrange a war between Prussia and Austria on one side, and little Denmark on the other, which Denmark naturally lost; and now he is planning another war, two years from now, between Prussia and

Austria, which Prussia will naturally win; and then. . . .

Besides the wars which are being fought or prepared, people in this year of 1864 are planning revolutions. Japan—which was dragged into the modern world just ten years ago by Commodore Perry's visit—is shortly going to have a civil war of its own, which will overthrow the powerful Tokugawa regent and make the emperor its ruler in fact as well as in name. In London, this very year, Karl Marx is founding the First International, to put into practice the dogmas of the Communist Manifesto, which he and Engels published sixteen years ago in 1848. In Russia three years ago the czar abolished serfdom; but something went wrong with that emancipation (as it did with ours in the United States) and Czar Alexander, like President Lincoln, will shortly be murdered. Interesting times; but difficult to live in.

Yet let us look at the other side of the year 1864. There is plenty of good reading, and more is on the way. Walt Whitman is working on *Drum Taps*, Dickens on *Our Mutual Friend*, Victor Hugo on *The Toilers of the Sea*, and Tolstoy on *War and Peace*. There is fine music in the air. Just a month ago, Richard Wagner, who was so disastrously in debt that he had to go underground to escape his creditors, was invited to Munich by the young king Ludwig of Bavaria. He has accepted with delight, and is taking with him the libretto for his greatest work. This very summer he starts to compose the music for *The Mastersingers of Nuremberg*.

And great world-changing enterprises are afoot for the benefit of mankind. In Egypt, the French promoter Ferdinand de Lesseps is building the Suez Canal to link the Mediterranean Sea with the Indian Ocean. In this country mail for California from the East is still being carried overland by pony express all the way from St. Joseph, Missouri, to Sacramento; but the surveying is now being done for the Union Pacific Railroad, which is to build westward from Iowa to meet and link up with the eastbound Central Pacific. (Most of the laborers on these railroads are Irish or Chinese; they have a regrettable tendency to blow one another up with carelessly placed charges of dynamite.) And this very year, in Cleveland, Ohio, a refinery has been opened to process a promising new source of power called petroleum. Its organizer is a young fellow of twenty-six called John Davison Rockefeller. Those who graduate in 1864 and go out into the world will do well to keep an eye on him. Yet he has contemporaries who will be less powerful, but surely more interesting. William James is soon to finish at Harvard: he will become the greatest psychologist ever produced on this side of the Atlantic. In France a twenty-three-year-old painter called Pierre Renoir is at art school together with two other ambitious young artists, Claude Monet and Paul Cézanne. And in the United States a young tramp telegrapher aged seventeen has just patented his very first invention, an automatic telegraphic repeater: his name is Thomas Alva Edison. Some nations give destroyers to the world, others give benefactors. On the whole, more benefactors than destroyers have come from the United States.

Let us go back another century. How do things look to the class of 1764?

Very different. Europe is in a condition of elegant decadence, and these American colonies in a state of rather primitive simplicity. We have a few colleges, but no university—while some of the European universities are already five hundred years old. In New York City, King's College (to be renamed Columbia in the future) is ten years old, headed by its second president, Myles Cooper. In Virginia George Washington is thirty-two, serving as a member of the House of Burgesses. He is a British subject, loyal to the young king George III; and, if we may conjecture what is in his mind, it is a feeling of patriotic relief and gratitude. For the long-sustained effort of the French to outflank the British colonies on the north in Canada and in the west along the Ohio River, which Washington personally investigated ten years ago, has just been ended forever by the Treaty of Paris, signed in 1763; and this part of the continent will remain English-speaking. Ben Franklin is living in London as a representative of the Colonies. Next year, when the idiotic Stamp Act is passed by Parliament, he will work for its repeal, speaking as a true British subject. The great sensation of this year in London, however, is not Ben Franklin, but a charming little Austrian boy only eight years of age, who plays the harpsichord exquisitely, and has composed something never heard of before, a sonata for four hands. This is Wolfgang Amadeus Mozart. Here among ourselves the class of 1764 will be small but distinguished. In particular, there is a serious young man studying law at Williamsburg. He is only twenty-one, but his character is already forming itself. Last year he wrote to his friend John Page a thoughtful letter, stating what he will continue throughout his life to maintain and practice:

Perfect happiness I believe was never intended by the deity to be the lot of one of his creatures in this world; but that he has very much put in our power the nearness of our approaches to it, is what I have steadfastly believed.* The most fortunate of us, in our journey through life, frequently meet with calamities and misfortunes which may greatly afflict us; and, to fortify our minds against the attacks of these calamities and misfortunes, should be one of the principal studies and endeavors of our lives. . . . Such, dear Page, should be the language of every man who would wish to render his situation in this life as easy as the nature of it will admit. Few things will disturb him at all: nothing will disturb him much.†

A good letter for a young man of twenty. It shows that he did not waste his time at the College of William and Mary. Mastering the fundamentals of Greek philosophy, he chose the one doctrine to which he was always to adhere, until the end of his life—the doctrine of Epicurus, which centered on *ataraxia,* spiritual calm.‡ It demonstrates the strength of his character. It does not show the versatility which he will develop. Later he will be known for his wide-ranging abilities, as one of the few men who can calculate an eclipse, survey an estate, tie an artery, plan an edifice, try a cause, dance a minuet, and play the violin. His name is Thomas Jefferson.

---

*In this can we not see the genesis of that great phrase "Life, Liberty, and the Pursuit of Happiness"?
†Jefferson, Letter to John Page, 15 July 1763.
‡Jefferson, Letter to William Short, 31 October 1819.

Now let us reenter the time-warp and imagine ourselves in the year 1664.

Looking around, we see those familiar spectacles, war
and despotism. King Charles the Second, recently restored to the lately united thrones of England
and Scotland, is getting involved in a war against
the Dutch. His people have led off this very year by
seizing a Dutch colony in North America, established
over forty years ago—rich forest and plain land, with a
huge, navigable river and a splendid natural harbor: the
colony of New Netherland, with its chief city of New
Amsterdam, now to be renamed New York. But apart
from that tiny territorial gain in a distant and barbarous
region, the war will be a disaster for the British. The
Dutch will sail right up the river Thames and sink some
of the Royal Navy in harbor. But King Charles will not
care, provided he has an inexhaustible supply of money
from France and pretty women from almost anywhere.
(Their illegitimate children will become earls and dukes
and inhabit some of the stately homes of England, despis-
ing people who have worked for their livelihood for
many productive centuries.) In this particular year three
remarkable young men are just entering on their careers.
The king of France, Louis, fourteenth of that name, still
in his twenties, has just rid himself of the wily Italian
chief minister Mazarin, and (with Colbert as his subservient grand vizier) is pronouncing those words so familiar to all students of absolute monarchy (whether in 1764
or in 1964): "The State is I." A handsome and intelligent
young French orphan, brought up to be a priest, has
gravely disappointed his aunts and uncles and spiritual
advisers by abandoning the church for the stage. This
very month, in June 1664, his first play is being produced

by the eminent director Molière: he is Jean Racine. And in England one of the chiefs of the Royal Navy is worried about a promising young son who is getting some peculiar notions about God, and the equality of all men, and the sinfulness of mankind. The youth is only twenty, and he is called William Penn.

The period that I know best lies much further back. For over forty years I have been reading the Romans— or should I say listening to them as they talk to me? I shall not say I fully understand them; but I find them sympathetic and intelligent and strong-willed, and far closer to us spiritually than the men of the Middle Ages. Like us, they built a huge, complex civilization, based on urban life, highly advanced in technology (they were remarkable engineers and road builders, unequaled until the nineteenth century) and depending on the exchange of goods and services over millions of square miles. Like us, they preferred a free republic to any form of monarchy and maintained the republican form of government, safeguarded by checks and balances, for many centuries —although at last the dictators (Julius Caesar being the first) managed to seize power and keep it. In one field they surpassed us. Starting from very crude beginnings, they developed a magnificent literature of prose and poetry, rich in imagination and subtle in expression, which at its best is far above the highest of our own achievements—to date.

Now, if you think our times are difficult, then imagine yourself back in the year 64 B.C. What faces our Roman contemporaries?

War, as usual. Pompey, a superb general in his early forties, is in Asia Minor crushing the last dangerous

enemy of Rome in the whole known world, King Mi-
thridates. As well as war, revolution, with the threat of
dictatorship. Julius Caesar (not yet known as a soldier)
has recently been connected with a formidable subver-
sive plot. Its leaders intended to murder the chief ex-
ecutives of the government, seize power, and declare a
revolutionary regime. This year's elections are bitterly
contested. On one side, the dangerous and rebellious
Catiline; on the other, a new man from an unknown
family, who has had a sensationally successful career
because of his genius as a lawyer and orator and his
ability as an administrator: Cicero. If Catiline wins, he
will institute a reign of terror and throw the whole of
Roman society into chaos. (In fact, he lost the election,
and a few months later was killed at the head of his
revolutionary forces.) Behind us in 64 B.C. lie no less
than seventy years of civil strife, stained by bloody dic-
tatorships both of the left and of the right. Ahead—and
the wisest of us (such as Cicero) gloomily foresee it—lie
thirty more years of intermittent civil war, broken by a
brief peace under the one-man rule of Julius Caesar and
resuming after his assassination (or, as Brutus and his
comrades called it, rightful execution). The peace-
maker, the savior of the world (as he will be called by
the men of his time), the future emperor Augustus, is
not yet born. Only a very strong nation can endure
such stresses without collapsing into blood and ruin;
and only a nation with inborn genius can at the same
time produce great art and literature. In 64 B.C. the
most promising contemporaries in literature are a
young lieutenant of Caesar's, called Sallust, who (after
retiring from politics with a large and dirty fortune)
will become one of the most incisive and cynical of his-

torical writers; and a sensitive young provincial from northern Italy, with the peculiar name of Catullus, who is to be one of the finest lyric poets of the Western world.

Now move forward to A.D. 64. The Greek and Roman world looks far more peaceful and prosperous and populous; but, in some important ways, far worse than before. Once overthrown, the republic could never be reestablished. It became a monarchy, at first in disguise, and then, more and more openly, an absolute monarchy. The Romans are now making the hideous discovery that, once lost, political liberty is all but impossible to regain; that every dictatorship tends to corrupt not only the dictator but his subjects; and that absolute power drives its possessors mad. In this year the young emperor Nero, aged twenty-seven, has been reigning for ten years, has murdered his mother, his wife, and his brother, and has cowed or demoralized or killed much of the social and intellectual aristocracy of the empire. As though to symbolize the destruction of ancient virtues and noble traditions, a huge fire in this very year destroys more than half of the city of Rome. For any disaster, a despot must find someone else to blame: so Nero accuses the Christians of setting fire to the city. They now appear for the first time on the stage of world history. The haughty phrases of the Roman historian Tacitus will tell the story.

Wrapped in the skins of animals, they were torn to pieces by dogs, or fixed on crosses and burned to illuminate Nero's park by night. The result was that, although they were worthless criminals, the people pitied them.*

The people pitied them; and the Christians who survived that first massacre venerated a place in Nero's park across the Tiber where the remains of one of their leaders, called Peter, were believed to be buried. That spot, marked with pious graffiti left by their successors, I have had the privilege of visiting, under the guidance of an official of the excavations conducted under the pope's authority. It is now buried deep beneath the center of the church of St. Peter. To descend the stairs, to creep along the narrow passage, and to see the tomb-chambers of those early Christian families who clustered around the hallowed shrine like bees around the queen, is like stepping back from 1964 to the age of the emperor Nero, across nineteen centuries.

Nineteen hundred years; but less than seventy generations. Your seventieth grandfather, if he lived in Europe or North Africa or Asia Minor, was a subject or an enemy of the emperor Nero; he was a contemporary of those early martyrs. Perhaps he even suffered among them; or watched them suffering, and pitied them, although he was intended to despise them; or else, in some distant province, he heard of their sufferings, and began to wonder whether, above the irrational rule of the young emperor who defied even his own gods, there might be some saner, some diviner law. That was a turning point in history, the year A.D. 64. It was besmirched by folly and polluted by vile cru-

---

Annals 15. 44.

elty; and yet it marked the birth of a new kind of civilization which, although strange at first and for long incomprehensible to many people, proved to be good,
and to offer one type of salvation—or at least relief—
for suffering mankind.

GILBERT
MURRAY

For many years he was the most famous classical teacher in the world. The most highly respected in his own profession: no. A dry specialist like A.E. Housman, a diamond-hard and many-faceted genius like Wilamowitz-Moellendorff, although less widely known to the public, stood higher in the regard of their colleagues. But for many years everyone in the English-speaking world who heard any mention of Greek poetry at once thought of Gilbert Murray: very much as everyone devoted to the history of painting and sculpture nowadays will think of Kenneth Clark. He became famous for a number of convergent reasons: because he was a superb teacher; because he translated Greek dramas into modern verse (modern for its time) and had them produced on the stage; because he played an active part in English politics; because he was a powerful advocate of the League of Nations during its hopeful beginnings; because he wrote fluently and gracefully on many themes, not all of them classical; because he talked well and often on the B.B.C.; because he was a friend of many distinguished people and an enemy of few; and because he had a peculiarly, almost uniquely charming, personality, full of grace and delicacy unexpectedly combined with an indomitable will and phenomenal physical vigor. As often as I met him, I never ceased to wonder that this mild-mannered man who neither smoked nor drank nor ate animal flesh, and whose soft, melodious voice, elegantly modulated and yet never sounding affected, was in perfect harmony with his clear blue eyes and his fastidious gestures, was in fact not a little brook sparkling and purling in a corner of the forest, but a noble river fed by many tributaries, sweeping along with steady surging power, nourishing many peoples and broad lands.

Gilbert Murray was an Australian. He was born in Sydney, the year after the assassination of Lincoln. (His father was born while Napoleon was still emperor of the French. It is astonishing to think that those two generations, father and son, should have seen both Napoleon and Hitler.) Murray was Irish through his father, Welsh through his mother. Not Anglo-Saxon, therefore, but Celtic: though he showed no signs of the Celtic tendency to fly to emotional extremes. He used to speak with much pride of his father, who went out to Australia as a very young man, a pioneer like the men who at the same time were exploring our western territories; became a sheep farmer in a big way; acted as sheriff, hunting down lawbreakers; fought hard to keep the natives ("blackfellows" or "abos") from being corrupted by unscrupulous white traders; at last became Speaker of the Legislature of New

South Wales and was knighted by the queen.*

When Murray was seven his father died; when he was eleven, his mother took him to England. There he was molded by the English educational system, which (reformed by the University Commissions of 1854 and 1877) was now beginning to offer "a career open to the talents."† He went to the Merchant Taylors' School: one of the senior English "public" (= really private, but nonprofit) schools, established by one of the ancient guilds of the City of London. He soon became an outstanding classicist, and easily won a scholarship to St. John's College, Oxford, which is connected with the Merchant Taylors' School by many ties.

When he went to Oxford he was the third son of an Irish immigrant to Australia who had made some money and some local distinction but was now dead. Apparently he was not connected with the English "establishment" by any of these ties of blood and tradition which made it then, and to some extent still keep it, one of the tightest aristocratic systems in the Western world. He was nobody in particular. But he had remarkable gifts of intellect and imagination, as well as the gift of making friends. In his first year he won the two most difficult classical competitive examinations in the university, the Hertford and the Ireland scholarships. This had seldom if ever been done before, and has perhaps never been done since. From then on Gilbert Murray had firm ground under his

---

*Murray's elder brother, Sir John Hubert Plunkett Murray, served as lieutenant-governor of New Guinea for over thirty years, and was also knighted, for his wise and resolute defense of the natives' interests.

†The phrase was coined by Napoleon.

feet. He rose, and went on rising till he was famous.

By the bye, he was not a narrowly ambitious scholar. He wrote original poetry. And he was a prominent speaker in the university debating society called the Union. There he was a pillar of the central, the intellectual, the ultimately unpopular but perhaps rationally right cause, the cause of the Liberal Party. Throughout his life he never ceased to be surprised and grieved that the Liberals in Britain (and indeed throughout Europe) were diminishing in numbers and influence and hopefulness. Liberalism he regarded as the central area between the two extremes of conservatism and radicalism. He felt it ought to have drawn the best part of the two antagonistic parties into the center. But in politics, as in moral life, *ought* does not mean *is*.

Within the classical field his special talent at this time was what the English paradoxically call "composition," meaning by this not the creation of original prose or verse, but translation from English models into Greek and Latin. The best schools and the two major universities of England have long specialized in this curious area of classical study, far more than those of any other country. Foreigners were always astonished to learn that schoolboys were taught to write Latin verses at the age of eleven (and beaten if they got the meter wrong) when they were not expected to compose poetry in English, and when (some foreign critics said) they would have been better employed reading more widely and discussing what they read. The system inflicted much unnecessary hardship on generations of pupils and sometimes gave them a permanent distaste for the classics. Yet when it succeeded—as it did with Murray and some others—it produced a marvelously sensitive appreciation not only of Greek and Latin poetry and prose, but

of the arts of poetry and prose in general: of literature.
Maurice Bowra, who died only the other day, was a
masterly "composer"—I treasure his transmutation of
Kubla Khan into a Greek ode in the manner of Pindar—
and this avocation did not prevent him from writing
sound and penetrating critiques of modern French and
German and Russian poetry, but, I feel sure, assisted
him. Gilbert Murray could produce Greek poetry more
easily than most people can write English. A friend of
mine once saw him, after breakfast, pick up the *Times*
and turn one of the editorials into Greek dramatic verse,
speaking almost at normal conversational speed. When
he returned from getting an honorary degree in Stock-
holm, he told me that the rector of the University had
startled him a little at the banquet by proposing his
health in an extempore speech delivered in Latin. "What
did you do?" I ventured to ask, knowing that he was
capable of many things. "Oh," he said with a guileless
smile, "I was so nervous that I replied in Greek."

Finishing off his undergraduate career, he aimed at
winning a fellowship in one of the Oxford colleges.
Such a post was the height of many young men's ambitions in the nineteenth century. It was only the opening of Murray's career, but it was difficult enough to
secure. It had to be won by competitive examination.
The brilliant and eccentric professor Margoliouth, one
of the examiners, asserted he was going to "set papers
which would try the powers of Murray of St. John's."
And so they did: enough to show that he was far above
his competitors. One of these tests would make most
modern classicists blench. It was to turn into Latin (of
course without a dictionary or any other assistance)
part of Walter Pater's essay on Luca della Robbia. Another of the candidates recalled for nearly fifty years

that particular passage and the graceful phrases into which Murray translated it.

These Tuscan sculptors of the fifteenth century worked for the most part in low relief, giving even to their monumental effigies something of its depression of surface, getting into them by this means a pathetic suggestion of the wasting and etherialization of death.

He won the fellowship at New College. Almost immediately, he went a long step higher. He became professor of Greek at the University of Glasgow. This was a greater honor than, to an American observer, it might seem. In the senior British universities there is only one professor for each subject (whereas a glance at an American university catalog shows me sixteen full professors in one department); there are no associate or assistant professors; the other teachers of the subject bear non-professorial titles such as reader or lecturer, far beneath the dignity of the professor. To reach such a position at the age of twenty-three was a special honor—made more special by the fact that in the post Murray succeeded Richard Jebb, who had just (aged forty-six) become Regius Professor of Greek at Cambridge. What would he do in it?

He was very good. He never wholly failed through his own fault at any undertaking to which he set his hand. There is a story that the moment he got the chair he set out to read through the entire corpus of Greek literature.* At the same time he wrote and published much,

---

*This massive enterprise has been accomplished by few scholars in modern times. Perhaps Murray approached it with a little too much

lectured eloquently, and spoke in public. But after ten years in Glasgow he suffered a complete breakdown, resigned, and, after a recuperative voyage round the world, returned to England. His doctor forbade him to teach, and enjoined him not to study as hard as he had been doing.

Now, Glasgow is a rough, ugly city; and the university, although it is a handsome group of buildings set on a hill in a beautiful park, cultivates few of the graces which are part of the very essence of Oxford life. In particular, the manners of the students have always been rowdy. In large classes they do not sit passively absorbing information, but banter the instructor, shuffle their feet loudly if he is obscure or inaudible, stamp on the floor in deafening unison to mark approval of a witticism, sometimes open the hour with loud choral singing, and generally try to dominate their teachers, rather than acknowledge their superiority. If a lecturer says: "I shall now run through the epidiascope," the announcement is apt to be greeted with the sound of clattering feet and hoarse panting noises; if he is unlucky enough to repeat one of his pet phrases, he will hear it chorused in accompaniment by twenty or thirty robust voices. It is all great fun—for the students. I went to Glasgow University myself, and I remember thinking that the freshman year, after the strict discipline of high school, was pure delight. The Latin class began at nine in the morning, and after a mile's walk in the cold rain to reach the university it was very jolly to greet a tardy lecturer with a chorus

---

confidence. He began one of his early books on the subject by saying: "To read and re-read the scanty remains now left to us of the Literature of Ancient Greece is a pleasant and not a laborious task." In the margin opposite this a crusty Cambridge don wrote *Insolent puppy!*

of *Oh, why are we waiting?* sung to the tune of "O Come All Ye Faithful." We had very little reverence for academic conventions. Once every year the rival parties in the student elections met in a pitched battle outside the main university building and showered each other and the terrain with rotten eggs, overripe tomatoes, decaying fish, and other malodorous missiles. The first academic procession I ever saw struck me, aged eighteen, as supremely ridiculous—all those old, bent, gray-haired men tottering along in sumptuously colored and elaborately embroidered robes and absurd hats with gold tassels, preceded by a beadle with his red nose and his gold mace. Delightedly, I joined a dozen of my friends in an impromptu snake dance which wove along beside the procession. When the principal of the university, the venerable Sir Donald MacAlister, fetched me a hefty blow across the shoulders with his gold-headed cane, I was honestly surprised. But this kind of rowdiness can very easily degenerate into bullying. I have myself seen a timid bespectacled young lecturer, made more vulnerable by what seemed to us an effete English accent, almost reduced to tears by a mob of several hundred laughing, shouting, jeering hobbledehoys whom he was vainly endeavoring to introduce to the beauties and subtleties of Vergil's poetry.

There is at least one story about Gilbert Murray's sojourn in Glasgow which implies that he was harassed by this disorderly atmosphere. Traveling south by train, on vacation, he shared a sleeping carriage with another man. Murray lay awake for a time, then slept, and (like so many teachers before and after) dreamed that he was lecturing to a difficult class. He delivered his opening sentences. They shouted at him. He attempted to continue. They roared louder and louder. (No doubt in his sleep he was hearing the unceasing racket of the train.) Finally, still asleep, he shouted out: "I will not have this noise. Be silent!" At once the stranger in the other berth woke up and said: "Was I snoring? I'm so sorry. I'll try to stop it. Good night."

This implication is contradicted by Murray himself. In his *Unfinished Autobiography* he says: "I liked my students immensely.... They were not at all rowdy, but did insist on being properly treated." As for his illness, he writes: "How impossibly hard I worked till, after ten years of it, my health rather gave way and I had to retire and recover." But he speaks as though it never occurred to him to go on sick leave and then return to his chair at Glasgow, although he was still in his early thirties. Instead, he settled down in the peaceful south of England, and when he resumed teaching it was not at Glasgow but at Oxford. In his letters to his young wife he wrote very differently about the Glasgow students. Meeting the junior class was "an awful strain—much more than I thought possible. . . . The whole work is Policing. You have, so I am told, never to look at your book, and never to look at one man for more than a few seconds. You keep your eyes wandering up and down every corner of the room, watching for insubordination . . . at present it sickens me . . . of course I shall beat them in the end, but it is such degrading work." In the end he did impose his authority, by his unusual combination of resolution and charm; but the effort was too much for him to sustain.

He can never have felt at home in Glasgow. All the more so because he had just married an English aristocrat, and had entered more and more strongly into the tradition of English Liberalism. This would not go down at all well with the heavily conservative middle class of

Scotland: "he was described as a socialist, a revolution-ary, a republican, an agnostic, an atheist."* It is a mistake to think of the English aristocracy as all composed of conservatives striving to preserve social, political, and financial oligarchy. On the contrary, they can be divided into conservatives, liberals, anarchists, and eccentrics. The groups who really matter are the conservatives and the liberals. Murray's wife was Lady Mary Howard, the eldest daughter of the ninth earl of Carlisle. By alliance with this family he put himself solidly inside the tradi-tion of the great Whigs, the Howards, the Stanleys, the Cecils; and inside other traditions as well.

The earl was an eccentric: a competent painter in the pre-Raphaelite manner, and a pessimist who expected other people to be either stupid or wrong. The countess, Murray's mother-in-law, was a much more formidable personage: daughter of Lord Stanley of Alderley; mag-nificent as a public speaker; devoted to numerous good causes, including Votes for Women, Home Rule for Ire-land, and teetotalism. She tyrannized all around her—except her husband, who would retreat into his own quarters and communicate with her, for a time, only by letter. There is a tale that she once commanded Gilbert Murray and another daughter's husband: "Stand up, my middle-class sons-in-law!" That tale is apocryphal, but the true stories told by her daughter Dorothy are less comical and more shocking. When Dorothy decided to marry someone her mother thought unsuitable, she sol-emnly cursed her. "She cursed all that was to be mine, my life, my children, my husband. I was to suffer the

---

*So J.A.K. Thomson on p. 249 of his "Gilbert Murray" (*PBA* 43, 1958).

deaths, the humiliations, the miseries and infidelities she
had suffered."* It would be mistaken to suggest that
Murray's ideals were formed by his mother-in-law: he
was a teetotaler and a partisan of women's rights and
Irish Home Rule long before he met her; but her firm
principles, converted in her beautiful daughter to what
Murray himself saw as "idealism, saintliness, and inward
fire",† surely contributed to strengthen his already
strong character and convictions.

He himself said that his marriage connected him with
another important English tradition, this one not chiefly
political but aesthetic: late nineteenth-century romanti-
cism, personified by William Morris and Burne-Jones
and others. While still an undergraduate he had become
known as a poet. As soon as he started teaching, he began
to write poetic translations of Greek verse, sometimes
reading them in his fine melodious voice to a class which
had been studying the originals; and then to publish
them and have them produced on stage, with such bril-
liance that he became "the most successful interpreter of
the great Greek plays that the English world had
known."‡ The style which he adopted was a blend of the
poetic manners of Swinburne and William Morris, with
some admixture of Tennyson: archaistic, flavored both
by medievalism and by the King James version of the
Bible; often vague and mystical where the Greek was
hard and precise; tinged with a sensuous love of allitera-
tion and of certain heavily emotional words and phrase

---

*Dorothy Henley, *Rosalind Howard, Countess of Carlisle* (London,
1958) 135.
†*An Unfinished Autobiography* 101.
‡So Dame Sybil Thorndike (*Unfinished Autobiography* 152).

patterns, which makes a striking contrast to his austere and puritan nature.

At the age of thirty-three, then, Murray gave up his Glasgow chair. Forbidden by his doctor to teach, forbidden also to study as hard as he had been doing, he retired with a pension to a country house in the pleasant south of England. While still at Glasgow he had written two original plays in prose, neither an outstanding success when produced. Now he began to turn Greek plays into English verse and to interest himself in the re-creation of Greek drama on the contemporary stage. This meant not only providing verses which could be spoken by actors without sounding pedantic (the idioms, the rhythms, the decorative effects must be English and not ancient Greek) but ensuring that the results were actable and advising on their production. That was the literary achievement for which Gilbert Murray first became famous. As far as I know, there were absolutely no existing English versions of Greek tragedy which were intended for acting and could be successfully staged in a modern theater. In 1877 Browning had brought out a version of Aeschylus' *Agamemnon*, of which the following is a sample.

> KASSANDRA: I say, thou Agamemnon's fate shalt look on.
> CHOROS: Speak good words, O unhappy! Set mouth sleeping!
> KASSANDRA: But Paian stands in no stead to the speech here.
> CHOROS: Nay, if the thing be near: but never be it!

No audience could endure this kind of thing. Murray gave people something far smoother and more continuously intelligible. Furthermore, many of the deep meanings of the great plays had not been explained in a way which the average theatergoer could grasp. "Many thousands who knew Euripides only as one of the blackest of the curses of the public school system realized for the first time from [Murray's] translations and criticism that Euripides was a great and kindling poet, and that the plays, being designed for the stage by a master of the theatre, were extraordinarily effective when acted."* Sybil Thorndike, queen of English actresses, recalled how, at a rehearsal, he opened up a world of imagination for her. She was to play the virgin goddess Artemis: an unsympathetic part, rather remote and chilly. He gave her something to strive for by saying: "Opalescent dawn: that is how (as Artemis) you must think and feel."†

Murray never forgot that the Greek plays were religious events. The religion they served has long since passed away: no point in reviving it now. But in translating and producing Greek drama Murray used the spiritual powers it released to create a strongly mystical effect which was almost equivalent to a religious experience. His audiences did not feel that the plays were about old departed gods and heroes. They saw them as conflicts of eternal ideals. Euripides' *Medea*, for example, is a somber tale of a strong and passionately loving woman driven into madness and crime by a man's selfish cruelty.

---

*John Masefield (Poet Laureate 1930–1967) in *Essays in Honour of Gilbert Murray* 64.
†*Essays* 71. "Enlightening," comments Dame Sybil, "but exceedingly difficult in performance" (*Autobiography* 158).

When producing it, Murray said it might have been written specially to support the crusade for women's rights.* But there is more than that in the play. When Sybil Thorndike took it to South Africa and Rhodesia in 1928 and 1929, she found that its emphasis changed. Medea's husband, Jason, who repudiates her, and King Creon, who banishes her, are Greeks; but she herself is a foreigner, an Asian from the Black Sea, a barbarian. In South Africa (where no Negroes were allowed to attend performances) the drama seemed to typify the struggle of primitives against cool, powerful, civilized, selfish people like Jason, a struggle bound to end in disaster. Perceiving this, the players acted *Medea* with new insight, new fire. Just after the First World War, when Murray was doing everything in his power to support the League of Nations and to reinforce the idea that any laboriously negotiated peace settlement is better than war, his translation of Euripides' *Trojan Women* was staged. The tragedy begins on the morning after Troy has been captured, its men slain, and its women enslaved; and it heaps suffering upon suffering. An old Cockney woman, a street peddler, took a party of her friends to see it. She told her neighbor Dame Sybil: "We saw your play, it was lovely; and we all 'ad a good cry and a nice walk 'ome over the bridge, and shrimps for tea to cheer ourselves up. Them Trojans was just like us, we've lost our boys in this blank-blank war, 'aven't we? That was a real play, that was, dearie." Murray was delighted when he was told of this: "another score for Euripides."†

---

*Essays 74.
†Essays 74 and *Autobiography* 164.

After living in the south of England for some years, Murray went back to teaching—not at Glasgow, no, but at New College, Oxford, where he had held his first position after graduating. Two or three years of this, and in 1908, at the age of forty-two, he was appointed Regius Professor of Greek. To many people this seemed an ideal appointment. But not to all.

In 1935 or so I did some post-graduate work in Greek palaeography with an elderly Oxford don. He knew the subject very well—so well that he was bored with it; or else he was bored with his pupils, for he made no concessions to our ignorance and showed no spark of human interest during our classes. He had taught Greek at Oxford for forty years or so. Although I knew how eminent he was and how much valuable work he had published, he struck me as a sour old pedant without a heart. It was only later, after he retired, that I realized what had soured him. His record was highly distinguished. Thirty or forty years earlier he had spent vast amounts of time and energy on producing an authoritative text of the Homeric poems. The first two volumes (the *Iliad*, on which he collaborated with a senior man) came out in 1902—the list of manuscripts alone occupies twelve pages; the second pair (the *Odyssey*) in 1908. Without any doubt he was a classicist of high repute and high promise. Looking back from this distance, we see that he must have expected to become Regius Professor, for he had done far more solid work than Gilbert Murray. But Murray was appointed. The Prime Minister who recommended his appointment was Herbert Asquith; and Asquith was, like Murray, an ardent Gladstonian Liberal.

All this happened long ago. I have no first-hand knowledge of the situation in Oxford in 1908. I loved and admired Gilbert Murray, and respected but rather disliked old T.W. Allen; but I can see now that he, and doubtless other Hellenists, believed they had a far better claim to that desirable position. It would be with a bitter sense of grievance that they settled down into the routine of being, for the rest of their lives, college tutors or provincial professors. And this grievance would not be diminished by Murray's extracurricular activities. "His interest in public affairs, in Liberal politics, in the higher education of women, took up a large and increasing portion of his time, involving him in letters to the *Times* and *Manchester Guardian* and attendance on committees, for he was always being put on committees. . . . There were some who murmured that he should stick more closely to his proper business, which was the teaching of the Greek language within the University of Oxford."* The strangest comment on this delicate situation came from Murray himself, in a letter written to his wife while he was being considered for the professorship.† "I am not fit for the Chair of Greek. . . . I am too diverse in my interests. I do not feel exactly ashamed in reviewing my work, but I see clearly that none of it is great or solid achievement. Nothing which would entitle a man to be called a great scholar." And then, generously, he mentions a man who, like himself, had become professor at a Scottish university when very young, and was even then producing an epoch-making edition of Plato. "I could work," he writes, "very well with Burnet."‡ But

---

*J.A.K. Thomson, p. 251.
†Cited by Isobel Henderson in *Autobiography* 148.
‡John Burnet (1863–1928), professor of Greek at St. Andrews University 1891–1926.

Burnet was not selected, and stayed in the remote little city of St. Andrews for the rest of his life.

The professors at Oxford and Cambridge have a curious position. They are officials of the university, but the actual teaching of the undergraduates is mainly done through the separate colleges. There is only one professor in each subject, and he may well limit his functions to giving the statutory number of lectures and attending the inevitable committees, reserving the rest of his time for research. It would easily have been possible for Murray scarcely ever to see any individual students and to spend most of his days in his own study. Instead of that he worked extremely hard to make himself, as it were, a focus of the life of the university. At the time when I knew him I thought this was admirable, but normal, and even conventional. It is only now that I understand what unremitting efforts Murray made and how valuable his work was. His opposite number in Latin, Robinson Ellis, was a rather repulsive eccentric, dressed in rusty black and wearing enormous black shoes curling upward at the toes, a notorious miser who left many thousands of pounds in his current account at the bank, learned and ingenious, yes, but scarcely a man to influence the young. Gilbert Murray and his charming wife made it their business to meet as many of the best undergraduates as their time would allow; and they invariably invited the new young classical dons to visit them in their home. Young men at the opening of their careers always benefit from associating with an older man who shows, by example and by advice, that he takes their work seriously and that he himself is not a divinity, heaven-high, but a striving scholar like themselves.

His lectures to undergraduates were always popular. Beautifully prepared and delivered with exquisite persuasiveness (I had almost said "friendliness"), they were never dry and were always enlivened—as most lectures are not—by glimpses of the unexpected, intellectually stimulating parallels brought in from his immensely wide reading. In the Harvard lectures of 1907, later published in edition after edition as *The Rise of the Greek Epic*, he startled his hearers by drawing elaborate parallels between the growth of the Homeric poems and the growth of the Hebrew scriptures, and pointing out that the book of Genesis, for instance, is made up of three easily distinguished documents with three distinct points of view. (Murray had learned Hebrew at Merchant Taylors' School.) A friend of Dr. Johnson once told him: "I have tried in my time to be a philosopher; but I don't know how, cheerfulness was always breaking in." In the same way even when Murray set out his learned arguments and proofs with every effort at *wissenschaftlich* rigidity, the warmth and charm of his personality were always breaking in.

In classical scholarship he was not one of those who cultivate pure research for its own sake and address an audience "fit though few." He would not spend years upon editing an obscure and third-rate poet—as his contemporary Housman did with Manilius, chiefly because the obscurities of the poetry and the corruptions of the manuscripts gave him good opportunities for demonstrating his intellectual acumen and advancing the art of textual emendation. Murray's most ambitious effort along this line was his Oxford text of Aeschylus. It was not well received. In old age he worked very hard (with the assistance of several more rigorously trained colleagues) to produce a new improved edition; but that too has now been superseded.

What he did best was exposition: not popularization, but lucid and eloquent explanation of the important facts and attractive fancies about an author, a genus, or a period. He was never dry; he was nearly always vivid; he enjoyed nearly all his subjects and communicated that enjoyment to his readers. Here his romantic nature sometimes led him to prefer a bold and strange imaginative reconstruction to a drier and more cautious interpretation of the data. For example, he went too far in accepting the theories of Frazer and the other Cambridge anthropologists, which postulate, in the prehistoric ages which lie just behind much of the best Greek poetry, a widespread cult of fertility devoted to ensuring increase in the crops, the stock, and the tribe; and his treatment of Homeric men and divinities in *The Rise of the Greek Epic* now seems to overemphasize the primitive elements in the *Odyssey* and the *Iliad*. Foreign critics also saw in him something of the amateurishness beloved of the English, who (they say) refuse to be relentlessly thorough, and do not mind changing their opinions even on important scholarly problems from time to time.* Thus Murray published a book called *Four Stages of Greek Religion*, which by its title implies something like a complete survey of the subject, divided into four essential phases; but when a new edition was called for, he produced *Five Stages of Greek Religion*, explaining very suavely that he

---

*No European scholar could possibly have included in his autobiography the fact that he had written a book in two days, as R.G. Collingwood (1889–1943) did when speaking of his book on Roman Britain.

had found "a gap in the story." This was at least candid; but to some non-English scholars it seemed immature and even irresponsible.

Nevertheless, it is scarcely possible even nowadays for anyone to read Murray's books without learning a good deal: the expert scholars get new insights, the unscholarly find much instruction in the essentials and much stimulus. He was more of a guide than an explorer: significantly, in his inaugural lecture at Oxford, he warned his hearers that "Greek" as a subject was too much for one man to handle, so rapidly was it expanding, and he explained that he should need much help even in keeping abreast of the innumerable discoveries which were being made. He was not chiefly an analyst, for at heart he believed that analysis destroys. He was a synthesist. He viewed the ancient world as a collection of fragments, and he set out to fit some of them together.

How about his translations of Greek drama? They are best understood when we recall that his professed purpose was to make the plays into something that could be appreciated by people who liked poetry and drama but knew no Greek. Therefore they had to be written in the style which English readers and audiences of that era found most appealing. They were period pieces. Inevitably, this meant that when new types of poetry were introduced, Murray's versions came to be disliked. In 1920 T.S. Eliot published a savagely bitter attack on them called "Euripides and Professor Murray." This came out in *The Sacred Wood* (1920), when Eliot was only thirty-two and had not yet issued *The Waste Land*. It is one of the most harshly critical judgments Eliot ever produced. Evidently it was part of his own struggle to form a new poetic style; but it sounds also as though it were imitating the shrill dogmatism of Ezra Pound. Speaking of the superb actress Sybil Thorndike, he says: "Her personality triumphed over not only Professor Murray's verse but her own training." He speaks of Murray's versions as having the "highbrow effect which is so depressing," and calls his style "a vulgar debasement of the eminently personal idiom of Swinburne." Then he goes into detail, designed to show that Murray uses two words where the Greek has only one (not "shadow," but "grey shadow") and that he adds images which are not in the original (not "losing the delight of life," but "the cup of all life shattered in my hand"*). He ends with the cruel verdict that "as a poet, Mr. Murray is merely a very insignificant follower of the pre-Raphaelite movement," and, having condemned him, buries him under the stony epitaph: "It is because Gilbert Murray has no creative instinct that he leaves Euripides quite dead."

This is much too severe. Against it we can set the testimonies of John Masefield and Sybil Thorndike and many thousands of delighted playgoers. The trouble with Murray's translations was not that they killed the original dead (like Browning's *Agamemnon*) but that they changed, and to some extent diminished, the Greek plays. Murray rewrote much of Greek drama all more or less in one single style: that is certainly illicit. Nor can I believe that these noble plays ought to be put into *rhymed* verse (except perhaps for the lyrical sections). The click-clack of rhyme halts the rhetoric. Milton knew this: in the preface to *Paradise Lost* he called rhyme "no necessary adjunct or true ornament of poem or good

---

Medea 226–227.

verse, in longer works especially, but the invention of a barbarous age, to set off wretched matter and lame metre"; and it was with grimly smiling contempt that, when Dryden asked if he might rewrite *Paradise Lost* with rhymes added, he replied: "Ay, ye may tag my lines if ye wish." And the style ought to be closer to Shakespeare or Milton than to Swinburne. Here, for instance, is a stanza from the last chorus of one of the strangest and loftiest of Greek plays, *The Suppliants* by Aeschylus (1038–1042): it is a description of the attendants on the goddess of love.

> Companioning their dear mother come Desire, and she who cannot be refused, the enchantress Persuasion; Harmony too shares in Aphrodite, with the whispers and the motions of the loves.

Now this is what Murray makes of it:

> For of Her comes the dumb heart that longeth,
>   And the soft word that fails not, though afraid;
> And the music of the world to Her belongeth,
>   And the whisper of a man with a maid.

This is far more monotonous than the original (*three* verses beginning with "And"). It contains one phrase which might be called a cliché, adapted from Proverbs 30:19, "the way of a man with a maid." To provide a rhyme for "maid" Murray added an almost meaningless phrase, "though afraid," which dilutes the force of the original by adding a qualification. Of course there is neither a man nor a maid in Aeschylus: only the personification "loves" or "passions," *Erotes.* Indeed in the Greek all the nouns are far more abstract than Murray's "dumb heart" and "soft word" and "music of the world" and "whisper." On the other hand, the rhythm is successful, for the original is a slow waltz sung by a group of girls: when we read the printed Greek words we may not appreciate that, but it comes through Murray's version. It was a vagueness learned from Swinburne that made Murray write "of Her comes the dumb heart," etc., which means that Aphrodite inspires or creates longing in men and women: whereas Aeschylus has a different picture, that of a queenly deity surrounded by her attendants who reflect various facets of her personality. Murray's versions of Greek drama are—like Fitzgerald's mild and melodious renderings of Omar Khayyam—alluring introductions to the Greek playwrights but inadequate as a guide to their work at its best and highest.

Murray's lectures on Greek themes and translations from Greek drama were only part of his versatile and busy life. He was president of the Society for Psychical Research: he himself had a remarkable gift for telepathy, which he would demonstrate to small and sympathetic audiences. With great discretion but with unflinching zeal he pushed the cause of women's rights, and sat as a permanent member of the council governing one of the four women's colleges at Oxford. He also served as president of the Society for Simplified Spelling. In this his interests coincided, as they did elsewhere, with those of his friend George Bernard Shaw.* He wrote wisely and persuasively on the subject, pointing out the unfavorable

---

*Shaw put him into one of his plays, Major Barbara. There he is easily recognizable as Adolphus Cusins, quoting Euripides in an English verse translation. Major Barbara herself is modeled on Lady Mary Murray, and the formidable Lady Britomart is surely her mother, the Countess of Carlisle.

contrast between languages which are not pronounced as they are spelled—such as English, French, and modern Greek—and languages which are, such as German and Russian. However, his chief nonacademic activity was as a Liberal in politics. In the United States "liberal" is often taken to mean "left-wing" and paired with "radical." Not so in Britain, where the Liberals were for long the party of the center. Murray disliked both the Conservative Party and the Labor Party on the ground that they were each devoted to furthering the interests of one particular class. In an address to Liberal candidates for Parliament he wrote:

> The great danger . . . is the danger of refusing to see light or listen to reason, of being blinded by prejudice, by self-interest, by class passion or by national passion, of contentedly doing injustice to the weak because they are weak.*

He was never a socialist, and he was very far indeed from sympathizing with Communism—which is one reason why he was sometimes scoffed at during the pink thirties. In particular he despised both Communists and Fascists for their blind adherence to unreasonable dogmas and their ability to ignore obvious facts. One of his own reminiscences bears this out.

> When I was a freshman at Oxford, an electrician putting in electric light at Hatfield [the great seat of

---

*"What Liberalism stands for," *Contemporary Review* 128 (1925) 681–697.

the Earls of Salisbury] was killed through touching
a live wire; and I was told by an enthusiastic politi-
cian that the line had probably been left uncovered
by the Conservative leader out of hatred for the
working class.*

(This amusing story has its obverse in a satiric quatrain
by Hilaire Belloc:

Lord Finchley tried to mend the Electric Light
Himself. It struck him dead. And serve him right!
It is the business of the wealthy man
To give employment to the artisan.)

Elsewhere he illustrated the power and fatuity of revolutionary idealism by telling how Mary Wollstonecraft,
walking with an English friend in Paris during the Terror, was expatiating with enthusiasm on the reign of
humanity and love which the Jacobins were introducing,
when she slipped and fell in the blood that was flowing
from the guillotine. It had trickled quite a long way over
the cobblestones.†

More important than Murray's work for the Liberal
Party was his share in the creation of the League of
Nations—both in helping to draft the Covenant and in
enlisting public support for the aims and methods of the
League. He was not a pacifist, and once wrote: "I do not
see how you can put an end to war by running away
from it."‡ He even declared: "Force has its due place, to

---

*P. 694 of the same article.
†*The Cult of Violence* (London, 1934).
‡*Then and Now* (Oxford, 1935).

support the agreed law against the lawbreaker, but it should not trespass beyond that sphere, and even there the use of it is an evil."* When the League of Nations failed—as the United Nations appears to be failing nowadays—he took it as only one further example of an important historical fact, often witnessed: that strong and ruthless men can often get what they want for a time, and that they can be overthrown only through violence.

The chief lesson taught by Gilbert Murray's life seen as a whole is his fundamental philosophy. It takes a good deal of reading among his voluminous works before his creed can be defined, but when it comes clear, it is a noble and humane set of beliefs.

In a fine essay written during the worst times of World War II, *The Anchor of Civilization* (Oxford, 1943), he enquires what is the cause of all the suffering which the world has been undergoing. One by one, he examines and rejects many of the usual answers. It is not lack of religion. Murray was not a Christian; and here he observes that the world has many religions but that it is difficult to claim that any one of them is entirely and exclusively true. It is not materialism: our ancestors in earlier ages were even more gluttonous and grasping than we are. It is not poverty—for rich nations often make war on poor ones. It is not the failure of the world to carry out any one political program, since all political programs are limited and imperfect. It is simply the lust for power, the urge to dominate. He glances with contempt at those nations who, like

* *The Cult of Violence.*

the Germans under Hitler, persecute and kill *ostensibly* for the sake of high-sounding ideals but *really* from the brute lust for power. And then, looking into the future after the end of the war, he rejects the idea that the Allies are fighting in order to establish the American or the British Way of Life, the Century of the Common Man, the Four Freedoms, or any such ideal, half-Utopia and half-advertising slogan. These things may come (says Murray) but they are none of them essential. What is essential is to establish the rule of law. International order; moral law.

It is a simple but good antithesis. Law is reasonable. War is unreasonable, but natural. Law must be created and imposed by human effort: it is an institution difficult to maintain, but the only one which will ensure peace and some degree of happiness.

Elsewhere, in *Then and Now* (Oxford, 1935), Murray compares the optimistic nineteenth century, in which he grew up, with the dismal twentieth century, and enquires wherein the difference lies. He finds it in the disruption of this age. In the words of Yeats,*

Things fall apart; the centre cannot hold;
Mere anarchy is loosed upon the world,
The blood-dimmed tide is loosed, and everywhere
The ceremony of innocence is drowned;
The best lack all conviction, while the worst
Are full of passionate intensity.

In our drama, debased and trivialized; in the coarsening of our taste encouraged by vulgar journalism; in the

*"The Second Coming," from *Michael Robartes and the Dancer* (1921).

fragmentation of the human soul, invaded and disrupted by extreme psychological theories; in the failure of art to preserve anything like a tradition—in all these Murray sees the rise of chaos. But what is the alternative to chaos? It is cosmos: a world order. How can such order be achieved and maintained? By respect for reason. By respect for law. By respect for principle. "No liberal persecutes."

Such, then, was Gilbert Murray. Among scholars there are discoverers; there are critics; and there are teachers. Murray made some discoveries and wrote some illuminating criticism, but his greatest work was as a teacher. And he did not confine his teaching to the field of the classics. He saw that the classical world is virtually meaningless if it is considered in isolation. It is merely an ingenious intellectual exercise to read about the Greeks and the Romans just because they existed long ago. Looking at the sufferings of the Trojan women three thousand years ago, we might, with Hamlet, ask: "What's Hecuba to us, or we to Hecuba?" Their tragedies are nothing to us unless they are somehow our own tragedies; and that is how Murray saw the Greeks and Romans. Their lives prefigure ours. In some ways they were inferior to us, in some ways superior, in all ways instructive. But in particular they are valuable to us because they made a prolonged effort to create a worldwide civilization based on peace and law and order; and that sense of law and order flowed from a noble vision of the soul and the universe as based on harmony, and wholeness, and reason.

QUOTATIONS

Both in conversation and in lectures, both in occasional essays and in serious books, Gilbert Murray was eminently quotable. Bertrand Russell, himself a brilliant talker and his friend for over fifty years, speaks warmly of his amusing fancies in talk. "He assured me once that there was an Oxford don who had reduced all jokes to thirty-seven proto-Aryan originals, and, when anybody made a joke in his presence, he would say: 'Yes. There is that joke.'" Once Russell called on the Murrays unexpectedly. When he asked if they were at home, the maid replied: "Well, sir, I think they're *probably* in—unless they're out." It turned out that they *were* in. Russell remarked: "Mary, your parlour maid is of the opinion that the laws of thought should not be applied to empirical material unless with great caution." "Oh, what an unkind thing to say!" replied soft-hearted Lady Mary; but Gilbert said: "I am glad to know that she has such just views."

"A few years ago a Bulgarian friend of mine, an intelligent public man, explained to me that many people thought British policy inconsistent, but that he saw that our every step was dictated by our deep-seated determination—to do what? To annex Constantinople!"

"I suffered greatly from fear in my teens and twenties." (Fear, Murray explains, of being hated.)

"My conscience, I confess, is nothing like what it was in its prime, when, unless memory deceives me, its beak and wings were rather a terror to the neighborhood."

Gilbert Murray:

The Anchor of Civilization (Oxford, 1943)
A Conversation with Bryce (Oxford, 1943)
The Cult of Violence (London, 1934)
"In defence of old age," *The Spectator*, 19 January 1934
"The spelling of English," *The Spectator*, 7 December 1936
Then and Now: the changes of the last fifty years (Oxford, 1935)
"What Liberalism stands for," *Contemporary Review*, December 1925

T.S. Eliot, "Euripides and Professor Murray," *The Sacred Wood* (London, 1920) 64–70
Jean Smith and Arnold Toynbee (eds.), G. *Murray, An Unfinished Autobiography with contributions by his friends* (London, 1960), containing "The Teacher of Greek," by Isobel Henderson; "The Theatre and Gilbert Murray," by Sybil Thorndike in collaboration with Lewis Casson; "Gilbert Murray and the League," by Salvador de Madariaga; and some briefer essays.
J.A.K. Thomson and A.J. Toynbee (eds.), *Essays in Honour of Gilbert Murray* (London, 1936).
J.A.K. Thomson, "Gilbert Murray," *Proceedings of the British Academy* 43 (1958) 245–270.

ALBERT
SCHWEITZER

He showed every sign of living to be a hundred. Had he done so, Albert Schweitzer would have reached the mark —still growling and grumping—in the year 1975. He was famous over much of the world for many decades. His middle life was heaped with honors, and crowned toward its close by the Nobel Peace Prize. Yet not many people understood him: chiefly because he was such a manifold genius that only those rare beings who inhabited the same spiritual Himalayas could fairly estimate his personality. "Talent," said Goethe, "builds itself in stillness, character in the stream of the world."* Schweitzer had both a strong character and multiple talents. He formed them by dividing his life between driving activity such as would have exhausted most men and lonely retirement dedicated to contemplation.

---

*Es bildet ein Talent sich in der Stille,
Sich ein Charakter in dem Strom der Welt.*

He was born in 1875. All his life long he was something of an exile. He was brought up in the tiny Alsatian village of Günsbach. The cities closest to Günsbach are Strasbourg, the capital of Alsace; the Swiss city of Basel; and the German university town of Freiburg. This means that many different intellectual and aesthetic impulses were felt there, such as could never impinge on anyone growing up in central France or the midlands of England. But Alsace was an unhappy country. Four years before Schweitzer's birth it had been annexed by the newly formed German Empire—after being closely tied to France for many generations; and it was treated with Prussian arrogance as a German-ruled colony, administered by officials appointed by the Kaiser in Berlin, not one of them born in Alsace. The young men (in due course including Schweitzer) were drafted for service in the armed forces of the German Reich.

In religion also Schweitzer was an outsider. His father was a Protestant pastor; but he himself says that most of the folk in his birthplace (Kaysersberg) were Roman Catholics; and prominent among his childhood recollections are tales of the collisions between the two chief forms of Christianity: the rival sects sometimes competed to use the same building. He himself through most of his career was not actively in communion with any organized Christian church. Indeed, he was rejected by at least one group of Catholics; and—although he loved to play the organ at religious services—he was always obdurate in refusing to join any church. Was that because he resisted accepting the authority of others, however eminent, however long established?

Even in language Schweitzer was two persons, or more. He had two mother tongues, French and German

—or, to be more accurate, the Alsatian dialect of German. He wrote books in "high" German (dialect-free) and apparently with equal ease in French. He stated that his family always spoke French and that he wrote his letters to them in French, but that he felt his own language to be Alsatian-German. Many years later one of his neighbors told a reporter that Schweitzer's fellow Alsatians regarded him with some coolness because— long after the restoration of Alsace to France in 1918—he still insisted on using the former German place-names. His brother, they noted, habitually spoke French.* This is a psychical factor often neglected in biographical studies. In what language does an important man or woman think, dream, talk to his closest friends? Djugashvili, who called himself Stalin, was a Georgian. His native tongue was utterly unlike Russian, and he himself always spoke Russian with a heavy foreign accent. Did he *think* in Georgian and translate his thoughts into the alien tongue? Kwamé Nkrumah, dictator of Ghana, was brought up speaking Nzima. He spent some formative years in the United States and in England, and when he attained power he spoke good English. But did he think in English, or in Nzima? And, whichever was his mental language, how did it affect his thinking?

In studying Albert Schweitzer's character we must emphasize this curious, though not unique, upbringing. He was a prominent member of a species which has been growing more and more common in this century: the Displaced Person. We inhabit an era filled with rootless wanderers, self-banished exiles. Many of them drift and

*S. Rosenberg, "The Man from Strasbourg," in *The Come As You Are Masquerade Party* (Englewood Cliffs, N.J., 1970).

drift all their lives long: after tearing themselves away from their families, they never put down roots again. Others—and of these Schweitzer was one—make for themselves a new type of life. Like those plants called epiphytes which have adapted themselves to extract water not out of the ground, like others, but from the air, so Schweitzer drew his nourishment not so much from a single national culture as from the rich atmosphere of Western civilization.

He was extremely well educated in a very wide range of subjects. It is not known whether his father and mother saw that he was a gifted boy: except that they did note his musical talent. They must certainly have observed that he was physically very strong, and that he had enormous psychical energy and intellectual curiosity. Such boys are best kept fully occupied. He himself recognized that he had a passionate nature, prone to feverish excitement—so much so that he never ventured to touch playing cards lest he might be seized by the lust for gambling, and at the age of twenty-four he gave up smoking, seeing it as a dangerous self-indulgence. All that energy and all that passion might well have pushed Schweitzer into follies or excesses. But instead, first his parents and then his uncle and aunt and lastly he himself turned that volcanic force into good channels, idealizing and sublimating what might have become stupid hedonism or bestial lust. That is one value of education which many of us overlook. We believe that it is meant to train the young for "social adjustment," for living harmoniously in a community. We forget that with some natures it is necessary to train the individual, and to develop his or her special abilities: such people may never be absorbed into any group, and yet be of great service to themselves and to mankind.

One further little fact about his youth, recorded by himself. Very early he was penetrated by the awareness of misery: not only human misery, but the misery of animals. He hated circuses. He detested zoos. He gave up fishing. Does that sound silly? If so, consider this, written by a man obsessed all through his life with killing.

A grasshopper poked his head out of the bottle. His antennae wavered. He was getting his front legs out of the bottle to jump. Nick took him by the head and held him while he threaded the slim hook under his chin, down through his thorax and into the last segments of his abdomen. The grasshopper took hold of the hook with his front feet, spitting tobacco juice on it. Nick dropped him into the water. . . .

And later—

He pulled up the sack, reached into it, and brought out one of the trout. Holding him near the tail, hard to hold, alive, in his hand, he whacked him against the log. The trout quivered, rigid. Nick laid him on the log in the shade and broke the neck of the other fish the same way. He laid them side by side on the log. They were fine trout.*

Even before Schweitzer started going to school, his father taught him music. He had a natural ear, and did not have to study harmony, which others have to approach like geometry, stage by stage from the simple to the complex. Touchingly, Schweitzer once wrote that "only in musical improvisation" had he ever felt himself

---

*Ernest Hemingway, "Big Two-Hearted River."

to possess "any creative ability."* Not in composition, which takes a disciplined effort and requires many revisions and long reflection. This is another paradox in his nature. Many of the great composers have been marvelous at improvising—Bach, Mozart, Beethoven, Brahms —but their major efforts were expended on writing music. Bach and Mozart composed easily and speedily, Beethoven and Brahms (apart from bagatelles and trifles) slowly, gropingly, even painfully; yet all their creative genius flowed from their minds through the pen to the music sheet. There it became permanent. Although Schweitzer could play the centuries-old music of other men, and could create his own music while sitting at the organ, he was somehow prevented from writing it down: perhaps because he revered the great musicians too deeply to compete with them.

After his father had grounded him in music, he was sent on to excellent teachers. Eugen Münch (a kinsman of the conductor Charles Münch) taught him the organ so well that he was able to give a solo recital at the age of sixteen. There were good schoolmasters in Alsace too: the boy learned Greek and Latin from a friend of the famous historian Mommsen.

It is a bewildering task to follow Schweitzer's higher education. He was doing so many different things at once. I cannot think of any modern scholar, indeed I can think of nobody except a few Renaissance phenomena (such as Leonardo and Politian), who was engaged during his formative years in tackling such a multitude of subjects and penetrating so far into them. Here we notice another principle in education which is nowadays

---

*Memories of Childhood and Youth, p. 22.

almost wholly neglected. This is the example of greatness in stimulating the young by competition, in giving them guidance when perplexed, and in passing on a tradition of high achievement. The central explanation of Schweitzer's versatility in youth is his profound and lifelong admiration for Goethe. He never possessed Goethe's talent for writing memorable imaginative poetry; but he tried hard to emulate Goethe in the depth and breadth of his thought, he devoted himself to music with the same intensity as Goethe did to lyrical and dramatic poetry, and like Goethe he endeavored to make himself a "universal man." In two ways he surpassed his model. Goethe had no interest in Christianity, whereas it was central to Schweitzer's existence; and Goethe was a self-serving and self-preserving genius who cast a cold eye on the world, while Schweitzer spent much of his life on giving himself unselfishly to others.

When he was young, his chief interests were philosophy and music, with theology a close third. Restlessly he roved around in search of good teaching and strong stimuli, attending not only the newly founded university of Strasbourg but the university of Berlin, and spending some time in Paris, studying the organ with Widor and the piano with a pupil of Liszt's while doing philosophy at the Sorbonne. At the age of nineteen he was compelled to do his military service, but met an officer who recognized his gifts and gave him light duty. On summer maneuvres he enjoyed the exercise and fresh air (which he said helped to make him robust), read the Greek New Testament which he carried in his knapsack, and meditated on the personality of Jesus—thus preparing for a book he was to write over ten years later.

He graduated in philosophy with a doctorate from

Strasbourg in 1899, his thesis being on a difficult subject, the religious philosophy of Kant. Thereupon he became a preacher at a local church, a position which paid him about $25 a month. This kept him going until he could graduate in theology also. Then in 1903, aged twenty-eight, he became principal of the Theological College at Strasbourg, thus increasing his income to about $500 a year. Now he was starting to pour out books on a remarkable variety of topics; but they were by-products of a process going on within his spirit. On becoming twenty-one he had solemnly resolved to give up his life to preaching, philosophizing, and making music until the age of thirty, and then, when he knew more clearly whether he had talent or not (!), to turn all his gifts to the service of humanity.

Some would have thought that by preaching and interpreting good music he was serving humanity very adequately. But his energy and his ambition (a selfless ambition) drove him on to other goals, although he did not yet know what they were to be. For a time he thought of dedicating himself to the care and education of orphaned children; he tried welfare work with tramps and ex-convicts. Neither of these fully satisfied him. From his childhood he had been filled with admiration for the missionaries who spread the Christian faith in foreign lands. And now, just as St. Augustine when wavering on the brink of conversion was precipitated over it by chance or Providence, hearing the voice of a child calling out two words (*tolle, lege*) which he interpreted as "Take up [the book] and read," so Schweitzer was directed toward his destiny by happening to read an article on the need of missions in the land called Gabon, then part of French Equatorial Africa, situated right on the Equator, painfully primitive and dreadfully unhealthy. He determined to go out to Gabon.

Here erupted another of those curious conflicts which often appeared in Schweitzer's career. He was not an orthodox Christian. Although he firmly believed that Christianity was a valuable religion, and although he had been preaching on Christian themes for years, he could not be accepted without question by the missionary societies. His book *The Quest for the Historical Jesus* was just coming out. In this he treated Jesus as a man, although an extraordinary man; he pointed out a number of mistaken or false statements which Jesus made to his pupils; and he discussed whether Jesus did or did not claim to be the Messiah, the divinely appointed king of the Jews. In view of this, Schweitzer would certainly not be sent to Africa as a missionary to teach the Christian religion. If he were to go at all, it would have to be as a physician. Therefore, at the age of thirty, he decided to qualify as a doctor. This decision initiated what he himself later called "a continuous struggle with fatigue." For six or seven years he followed several careers at once: preaching, lecturing on theology and philosophy, and performing as a concert organist. At the same time he was studying medicine. He was successful, for his physical stamina was remarkable and his will unbreakable. Still, it was a hard struggle—one of those struggles which are designed to make strong men even stronger, for later tasks they can scarcely foresee. He graduated as a doctor of medicine in 1911 at the age of thirty-six. The thesis which he presented to the examiners dealt with the question of whether Jesus suffered from paranoia.

During 1912 he collected money and equipment to start

a hospital, and in 1913 he sailed for Africa. Two peculiarities appear in this important event. One is that Schweitzer was a German subject, but chose to establish himself in a colony of France. There were German colonies in Africa which needed help in the form of missions. While Schweitzer was preaching in Strasbourg, the Herero tribe of German Southwest Africa rebelled against German rule, and were firmly, indeed savagely, suppressed by General von Trotha. Surely the survivors required medical care and spiritual comfort. Furthermore, Schweitzer himself later wrote that he had known for years that a war between France and Germany was approaching: so he was aware that he would find it difficult to work in a region dominated by the French. Why did he select French Gabon? There is no pragmatic answer. In dealing with such a man it is always best to search for an idealistic explanation, and there is one at hand. He wished to teach, by example, that national boundaries and divisions between peoples ought not to exist: to show, even at the cost of his own career, that they are absurd.

The other peculiarity about his missionary journey is that he chose to start it on Good Friday. People do travel on Good Friday, but devout Christians do not, except in case of urgent necessity, and it is not shown that there was any urgent need of fixing such a day for the start of a long voyage. He records the fact himself, so that he must have thought it significant. Surely it signified that he did not believe in the divinity of Jesus; and also that he admired Jesus as a man—for Good Friday, the anniversary of Jesus' death, was the day on which Schweitzer believed he was to die to his old life.

Before his missionary work began he had published

three remarkable books. One was his *Quest for the Historical Jesus*. A second (originally written in French, then rewritten in German and expanded) was *J.S. Bach, Poet-Musician*, which treats Bach not as a monument of cool control and quasi-mathematical reason but as a vividly pictorial and delicately emotional composer. The third was an analysis of the architecture of organs in Germany and France, which denounced the highly colored sound systems that contemporary organ builders were introducing, and advocated a return to the pure and plain style of organ construction and organ playing. Schweitzer is too complex a character for most people to comprehend.

He reached Gabon in April 1913, aged thirty-eight. Apparently he meant to remain there for the rest of his life. But he did not. Even from the place of his exile, he was often exiled. The First World War broke out before he had been there eighteen months: his work was disrupted, he was interned, and finally in 1917 the French shipped him back to an internment camp in Europe.

When the war ended, Schweitzer did not at once return to Africa: whether because the postwar inflation made it impossible to finance his hospital, or because he had books to produce that could not be written in Africa, or because he felt he had to live for some time as a European musician, or because there was much suffering in Europe which it was his duty to alleviate. It was only in 1924 that he went back to Gabon. He had to start his work all over again. Most of the buildings had collapsed; the paths between them were covered with jungle; and there was no labor force, since the men were all in the forest cutting timber for export. Yet, with will power and faith, with vast expenditure of his own physical strength, and with his remarkable gift for convincing and dominating primitive folk, he built a new hospital; and then, in 1926, another and larger one up the river at Lambaréné.

But thereafter he returned to Europe once more: this time for two years of lecturing and giving organ recitals. He was back in Africa in 1929, and back in Europe in 1932. This pattern he followed through much of the rest of his life. Thus, he spent October 1934 to February 1935 in Europe, then passed seven months in Lambaréné, and then sought Europe once again. He was therefore not a permanently settled missionary. He had little interest in Africa, did not care for exploring, never visited Brazzaville (capital of the Belgian Congo, three hours away by air), spoke no African language, and did not in any sense share the life of the Gabon people. Although it is difficult to explain this bipartite existence, it was obviously good for Schweitzer. If he had stayed permanently in Africa with only an occasional furlough for rest and recuperation, he would have died too soon. His visits to Europe were not vacations but changes of life-style. They were anything but rest cures. The moment he landed, he used to ride off into a tornado of activity, traveling, lecturing, concertizing, and answering thousands of letters. Most people manage their lives comfortably by following a single routine with occasional interruptions at holiday time. Schweitzer lived best on a pattern of extreme contrast, ranging back and forward between witch doctors and cathedrals, cannibals and concert halls, lepers and lecture platforms. Winston Churchill used to say that he got the best relaxation not from physical rest (though he was devoted to his cozy bed) but from engaging wholeheartedly in some activity quite different from his regular tasks. Schweitzer's pattern went deeper than that. The stimulus he needed was only to be found in a range of variations too extreme for any normal man to endure without disruption. What inner conflicts that stimulus may have helped to control and harmonize, we can never know. Perhaps he himself did not fully know: for in *The Quest for the Historical Jesus* he wrote: "Progress always consists in taking one or the other of two alternatives, abandoning the attempt to combine them"—yet he contrived all through his long life to combine widely separate and apparently irreconcilable ways of living.

A long life, and a fruitful one, ending in 1965, when he was ninety years of age. No one could say that his character and work went unappreciated. It would take pages to tell of the honors he received—next to the Nobel, he was most moved when the city of Frankfurt awarded him the Goethe Prize—and of the disciples he made and of the articles and books written about him. These are external things. More important in understanding Albert Schweitzer is the group of master ideas which guided him through that complex and difficult career.

One of these is historicism. He refused to see persons and events and activities apart from their historical background, claiming that they could be understood only within their own context. In music, for instance, his chief aim was to play Bach as Bach heard his own music, with no modern additions. "The Cantatas and the Passion music were written for choirs of 25 to 30 voices and for an orchestra of about the same size."* It is therefore improper to have them rendered by a choir of over a

*Out of My Life and Thought, p. 66.

hundred voices with a large modern orchestra. Furthermore, "Bach did not use women's voices for alto
and soprano, but boys' voices only, even for the solos.
Choirs of male voices form a homogeneous unit."
Thus Schweitzer would discard female singers and introduce boys, not principally on the aesthetic ground
that boys' voices are sweeter and more limpid, but on
the historical ground that this was Bach's own practice. Also, he insisted that Bach's music was generally
played too fast—not necessarily too fast for good
taste, but faster than Bach himself played it. Similarly
Schweitzer's work on organ building was a protest
against the heedless modernism which likes anything
new and loud and striking, whether or not it wrecks a
good tradition.

In analyzing the thought of Jesus and of St. Paul,* he
treated the Gospels, with the Acts and Paul's letters, as
documents firmly rooted in history, recording what was
actually said and done. Most Christians believe that Jesus
was God, temporarily incarnated in the shape of man:
that he was the Second Person of the Trinity, with a
human body which could hunger and thirst and suffer
pain, but with a divine all-knowing spirit. I myself have
never been able to understand how this belief can be
reconciled with the last words of Jesus as recorded by
Matthew and Mark. Just before he died, he shouted out
the first words of the twenty-second Psalm: "My God,
my God, why hast thou forsaken me?"† Can God forsake
God? For Schweitzer, however, the problem lay not in
these words, but in the fact that Jesus made a number of

---

* *The Mysticism of Paul the Apostle* (1930).
†Matthew 27:46; Mark 15:34.

prophecies which did not come true.* Schweitzer therefore concluded that Jesus was a wholly human being, and
explained the mistaken prophecies as arising from the
mentality which, as a Jew of his historical period, he
would necessarily possess.

There is another master idea which helped to mold
Schweitzer's thought and life. This is dualism, or polarity. He had two languages (the languages of two national
enemies). He had a dual career, split between primitive
Africa and civilized Europe. He led two distinct and
irreconcilable spiritual lives: as a rationalist and as a
mystic. He often praised rationalism: indeed, some
would say that his analysis of Jesus' mental processes was
too coldly logical. He constantly stressed the idea that
Christianity was valuable only in so far as it could be
explained by reason: it did not, he said, rest on divine
authority or on the tradition of any single church; it was
a creed to be understood and accepted by everyone who
could think clearly.

Yet at the other extreme Schweitzer was a mystic. He
believed most firmly that the central principle of our
existence in this world ought to be *Reverence for Life*. If
we subject this principle to simple analysis, it dissolves.
Reverence for life; yes, but for which forms of life? No
rational answer is possible. If it means that we should
not kill or injure living things, then we give up eating
meat and fish; but we also abandon eating grain and

---

*He told his pupils that they would be persecuted on their mission-
ary journey, and they were not: Matthew 10:16–20 and Luke 10:1–20;
and he declared that before they had finished their mission the Messiah would come, but instead he was crucified: see Matthew 10:23 and
Mark 9:1.

vegetables and fruit, since they are indubitably alive until we cut them down or pluck them, and something of their life remains in them even when they are cooked. Therefore, if taken rationally and applied logically, the principle compels us to live on nothing but milk. I wonder whether this dogma was suggested to Schweitzer by his researches into Indian religion. There is one sect, the Jains, whose main doctrine is *ahimsa, Do Not Hurt.* When out of doors their holy men sweep the ground in front of them so that they may not kill any creature by stepping on it, and cover their mouths and noses with cloth to avoid breathing in any tiny insects which would die by being inhaled. They have hospitals for old and diseased animals, and feed them until they die. But here "animals" surely means only harmless herbivorous animals, and not cobras or tigers or wolves or any of the carnivores.

We may well criticize *Reverence for Life* on the ground that it destroys the qualitative system on which civilization is built. A child's head is infested with lice: must we not remove the lice? yet they cannot live if detached from a host. Many mosquitoes carry malaria and yellow fever: must we not exterminate them lest we ourselves die? Even by screening them out of houses and denying them their diet of blood we are killing them by starvation. And there are uncountable myriads of simple creatures, invisible but alive, which are parasitic on mankind, and which we *must* kill, or else either die ourselves or live in pain and deformity. These are the micro-organisms: the pneumococcus, the vibrio of Asiatic cholera, and so many more. They too are part of the great chain of being: they are alive and marvelously active and incredibly versatile and, many of them, desperately destructive to animals and human beings. Which life are we to revere? the life of the tubercle bacilli eagerly multiplying within the lungs of a child, or the life of the child? Had the question been put to Schweitzer in that simple but logical form, he would have brushed it aside. After all, he ran a hospital: every day he was showing his reverence for one form of life by destroying other forms of life. But the doctrine cannot be rationally discussed. It is a nonlogical concept, and it emerged from the mystical side of Schweitzer's nature. Although he never claimed to be in communion with the divine, he was a mystic of the universe. He himself acknowledged the duality of his nature. One of his difficulties in carrying out a process of logical reasoning (he said) was that he was likely to be interrupted by dreams and visions. If he ever saw a ray of light broken up into prismatic colors by passing through a crystal he was apt to enter another world, in which there was no room for rational thought.

One further, and higher, example of the polarity within Schweitzer's spirit. He was disliked, indeed rejected, by many religious people for his insistence on examining the records of Jesus' life with the eye of reason, criticizing them for what seem to be inconsistencies and correcting their interpreters for what he judged to be faulty explanations. His attitude to Jesus was, it would appear, one of sympathetic but unbending rationalism.

Yes, but that is only part of his attitude to Jesus. Was not much of his life spent in the mystical imitation of Jesus? What else could be meant by his long sacrifice of his strength and his talents for the sake of people whom he did not particularly like and who were not even sub-

jects of the country of which he was a citizen? He himself
wrote: "The effort to serve the love preached by Jesus
may sweep a man into a new course," and went on to
describe such a course as "to popular logic non-
rational."* His most famous book, in which this saying
occurs, has a peculiar appearance, which reflects the
unusual structure of his psyche. It is printed as though
it were two books interwoven: the sections expressing
Schweitzer's thoughts are set in a type different from the
main body of the work. Between the two there is an
organic connection, but nonetheless there is an emphatic
difference—as if his life, his career, were one activity and
his thought another, the two forming a polar duality
which only a great soul could unify.

A great soul? There were many who criticized him
bitterly while he lived. They denied him greatness, and
(as far as they think of him at all) they still do.
They call his philosophy shallow. He wrote far too
much, they say, so that any original ideas he may have
had came to be spread out so thin as to be worth little.
He was not, they declare, a philosopher, but an uplift
merchant. This criticism seems to me to be partly justified. I cannot find that Schweitzer cast any fresh light
on any important philosophical problem (his work on
the history of Christianity is on a different level); I do
not find anthologies of his philosophical cogitations
very stimulating; and sometimes they sound quite vacu-
ous. It would be easy to give examples, but one will be
enough. No one but a nineteenth-century German philosopher could seriously write down such a sentence as:

*Out of My Life and Thought, p. 37.

I recognize it as the destiny of my existence to be obedient to the higher revelation of the will-to-live which I find in myself.*

Are we therefore to put him down as a man who tried to become a philosophical thinker and who failed, perhaps through failure to concentrate? Was he like the majestic river in the poem? At first it flows

Brimming, and bright, and large: then sands begin
To hem his watery march, and dam his streams,
And split his currents; that for many a league
The shorn and parcell'd Oxus strains along
Through beds of sand and matted rushy isles. . . .†

No. That would be an unfair comparison. If he made no philosophical discoveries, at least he told the world some things which it has not been told often enough and still refuses to accept wholeheartedly. He should therefore be regarded not as an ineffectual philosopher, but as an effective teacher. In the world of thought that is his real claim to fame.

Other critics, very vocal during his lifetime, asserted that he was a magnificent success, not as a martyr to duty, but as a self-advertiser; that his frequent journeys to Europe and his lecture tours were worthless compared with the hard, unremitting, dutiful, silent work of real missionaries, who remain longer in their missions and talk less; and that his entire career could be explained as a masterpiece of carefully handcrafted public-

---

*Ethics, p. 257.
†Arnold, Sohrab and Rustum.

ity. Now, there is a fraction of truth in this also. Schweitzer accepted many honors. He lectured very freely. He published many books. He kept up a voluminous correspondence: authors who shun publicity never answer letters from strangers. Everything he said or wrote conveyed the vigorous imprint of his personality. But this criticism overlooks one fact: that he gave nearly everyone who knew him the impression of greatness. Yet, if he was great, why should he appear to advertise himself so consistently and so purposefully? The explanation goes deep into his youth and upbringing. He was the son of a pastor. As such he felt it his duty to be an *example* to others. All his missionary work and all his lecturing were designed not primarily to make Albert Schweitzer famous, but to persuade others to follow his example. In this he succeeded, at least in some degree. He caused thousands to think of self-forgetting service who would not have thought of it without his words and his deeds; he made them conscious of their duty to primitive people; and in an age when foreign missions are little regarded he kept the ideal of missionary service not only active but embodied in a heroic figure.

A third criticism was heard even while the award of the Nobel Prize was being acclaimed. This was a harsh one. Schweitzer (said these critics) did not understand Africa. He considered the Africans to be animals in human form; and his much admired hospital was a monument of out-of-date medical method. John Gunther told me it was the dirtiest place he had seen in the whole of Africa, "and you can imagine what *that* means." He added: "Schweitzer bosses the natives about just as though they were—" and then he stopped himself, as though he were about to use the dreadful word "slaves."

Norman Cousins describes it in carefully veiled terms, but still frankly enough.

> Countless numbers of goats wandered at will all over the place; even when they were not visible their presence was perceptible. The ground was made moist and slippery by an equally large number of chickens. Hanging heavily in the dank air was the smoke from the dozens of crude burners used by the Africans for their cooking. . . . The sanitary facilities were at an absolute minimum. There were only two outhouses, one for each sex. The sewer underneath was open and sometimes the wind blew from the wrong direction.*

Mr. Cousins also comments on the brusque manner with which Schweitzer treated Africans; but he adds that Schweitzer could be and frequently was gruff to everyone, black or white—partly because, after so many years of experience, he *knew* what should and what should not be done; partly because he always had a fanatically strong will, which would not brook opposition from others or from within himself. Although Mr. Cousins does not touch on it, I conceive that there may have been a third reason: that Schweitzer spoke none of the native languages. When one cannot explain and persuade in a man's own tongue, one tends to shout at him.

Criticisms something similar were leveled against the Belgian priest Father Damien (1840–1889), who went as a missionary to the Hawaiian leper settlement of Molokai and there died of leprosy. Soon after his death, a Protes-

---

Dr. Schweitzer of Lambaréné, pp. 91–92.

tant missionary wrote that he had been "a coarse, dirty man, headstrong and bigoted." This evoked from Robert Louis Stevenson an open letter which is one of the world's masterpieces of righteous invective. It did not squelch the Reverend Dr. Hyde of Honolulu,* but it built up "the image of a man, with all his weaknesses, essentially heroic, and alive with rugged honesty, generosity, and mirth." The attacks on Damien were evoked by religious jealousy sharpened by feelings of personal inadequacy. Those directed against Schweitzer had a different origin. Sub-Saharan Africa is a sensitive area. Schweitzer's view of Africa and the Africans was one which was and still is highly unpopular with many people. It is expounded at the end of George Seaver's excellent biography.† Put briefly, it is this. Since the Africans cannot—in the present state of world trade and world communications—be isolated and permitted to continue living as they have lived for many millennia, we owe it to them to teach them, to guide them, to help them. Schweitzer believed not in commercial and political colonialism, but in what might be called cultural colonialism. Now, if one were on principle opposed to colonialism of all types, if one held that the Africans could and should be left entirely alone to work out their own destiny; or alternatively if one believed that there was no difference in cultural levels between racial groups, so that any attempt by one society to "improve" another society could only destroy its innate values, thus doing

---

*By coincidence, Stevenson had several years earlier created a monstrous villain called Mr. Hyde (1886): this was before he ever visited the South Seas.

†*Albert Schweitzer, the Man and His Mind.*

harm and not good—then one would see Schweitzer as
a busybody, a tyrant, a corruptor rather than a civilizer.
There are people who think along those lines, although
their practice does not always follow their loudly pro-
claimed principles. From them came most of the really
vehement criticisms of Schweitzer. Some of them
conceded that he might have done some good, but added
that he did it for the wrong reasons. Others claimed that,
while pretending to do good, he did little but harm.
The gulf between Schweitzer's admirers and his de-
tractors can never be bridged: at least during our lifetime. Africa is rapidly evolving, painfully changing. In
some generations, perhaps several centuries, when it has
entered a new (so far unforeseeable) phase of development, it will be possible to appraise the work of Albert
Schweitzer. At present we can be sure of one fact: that
he was a remarkable teacher, a teacher for the world.

Albert Schweitzer:

> Out of My Life and Thought (tr. C.T. Campion, Holt, New York,
> 1949).
> Memories of Childhood and Youth (tr. C.T. Campion, Macmillan, New
> York, 1950).
> An Anthology (ed. C.R. Joy, Black, London, 1952).

N. Cousins, Dr. Schweitzer of Lambaréné (Harper, New York, 1960).
A. Hagedorn, Prophet in the Wilderness (Macmillan, New York, 1947).
C.R. Joy and M. Arnold, The Africa of Albert Schweitzer (Harper, New
    York, 1948).
G. Seaver, Albert Schweitzer: the Man and His Mind (Harper, New York,
    1947).

JESUS
AND HIS
PUPILS

I

After Socrates had been sentenced to death, he was kept
in prison for a month, while an Athenian embassy was
away on a religious mission. Friends and pupils were
with him every day. They came to the prison each morning before sunrise, were admitted as soon as the gates
opened, and spent the daylight hours talking with him.
One of them offered to help him to escape into exile, but
he refused. At last the embassy returned, executions became lawful once more, and Socrates prepared to die. He
spent his last day with his friends, discussing the immortality of the soul. Then he took a bath (to save the women
the trouble of washing his corpse), said good-bye to his
wife and sons, sent them away, and drank the cup of
poison. His friends burst into tears, but he reproached
them and they quieted down. A few minutes later, while
they watched, he died as calmly as he had lived.

The story is told by Plato in two short books called *Crito* and *Phaedo*. They give a powerful picture of Socrates' unique personality, and of the devoted love, loyalty, and understanding of his friends for "the noblest, the wisest and most upright man they had ever known." And they make a curious contrast to the tale of the last days and nights of Jesus. The sufferings of Jesus were far more prolonged and intense than those of Socrates; but the behavior of his pupils and friends, as described in the Gospels, was more selfish and unfeeling than that of the friends of Socrates.

One incident is particularly painful. After the Last Supper, knowing that he was soon to die, Jesus left Jerusalem to spend the night outside the walls, and went to a garden called Gethsemane. Of his twelve chief pupils he took with him only the three whom he had first chosen, and who were often close to him at great moments: the three fishermen: Simon called Peter, and James and John, the sons of Zebedee. He told them he was in deep sorrow, and asked them to stay awake with him. Then he went aside a little way and prayed God for mercy or for strength. When he turned back to Peter and James and John, they were fast asleep. He reproached them, and prayed once more. Once more, and yet a third time, he found them asleep. Now he woke them with an ironic rebuke: "Sleep on." But by this time the forces of authority had entered the garden to arrest him. After a brief show of resistance all the pupils of Jesus ran away.

So stands the story in the Gospels: Matthew chapter 26 and Mark chapter 14. It contains at least one difficulty. Jesus (we are told) prayed three times, and his actual words are given. Yet if Peter and James and John were all sleeping, who was there to hear, remember, and record his words?

Perhaps the answer is that his pupils heard him begin the brief supplication, and then, as he repeated it again and again, fell asleep.

During the last hours of Jesus we hear nothing of his pupils, except in the Gospel of John. In the other Gospels they are not even mentioned. His cross was not carried by one of his closest friends, but by a man from North Africa. His crucifixion was watched by some loyal women (including the mother of James and John) but not by the disciples. It was not one of the Twelve who obtained permission to bury the body, but the rich and influential Joseph of Arimathaea.

The contrast with the pupils of Socrates is obvious. In one way, it is explicable. Socrates had been tried and sentenced with due process a month earlier. When the time came for him to die, tempers had cooled down. His friends were not in danger of being arrested as his accomplices. Even the warden of the jail was sympathetic, and said good-bye to him with tears in his eyes. In Jerusalem, on the other hand, sympathies were sharply divided, passions were high, the authorities were afraid of a riot, and there was a general atmosphere of turbulence. It was natural enough for folk like simple fishermen from Galilee to fear the whole apparatus of wealth and power: one of the Twelve actually defected.

Yet when we consider the conduct of the pupils of Jesus, there is more to think about than a panic lasting only a few days. Most of us read the Gospels in order to follow the career and teaching of Jesus himself. If, however, we read them paying special attention to the behavior of his pupils, we shall be forced to conclude that they were an unsatisfactory lot. He scolds them far more often than he praises them. While Socrates is shown argu-

ing gently and painstakingly with his disciples and at last
convincing them through the power of reason, Jesus
again and again expresses his displeasure and disappoint-
ment.

Peter got the brunt of it. When he saw Jesus walking
on the water he volunteered to do the same, but began
to sink. Jesus saved him, and commented: "You have too
little faith." Not long afterward, when Peter was the
only one of the group to declare him the Messiah, Jesus
was pleased, and blessed him, and promised him the keys
of the kingdom. And yet within the same context (Matthew 16:21), when Jesus explained that he was bound to
go to Jerusalem and suffer death, Peter took it on himself
to protest, and in return got the shattering rebuke: "Get
behind me, Satan!"

The other two leading disciples, James and John, were
scolded too. Either they themselves (Mark 10:35) or their
pushy mother (Matthew 20:20) asked Jesus to give them
specially distinguished positions in the kingdom of
heaven. Jesus replied that such arrangements were made
by God. It was tactful, but it was an unanswerable repri-
mand, and the rest of the disciples were angry with their
ambitious colleagues. (According to Luke 22:24 the argument about precedence in heaven, with Jesus' reproach-
ful comment, occurred during the Last Supper: a more
painfully inappropriate time could scarcely be imag-
ined.)

Jesus made no effort to conceal the fact that he was
sometimes disappointed in his pupils. He said that they
lacked faith. He even said that they lacked intelligence.
A man with an epileptic son asked him for help, saying
that his disciples had failed to cure the boy (Matthew 27).
Jesus spoke angrily of the "unbelieving and perverse

generation" among whom he lived, cured the boy, and told his disciples they had not enough faith. Once he gave them advice in a metaphor, telling them to beware of the leaven of the Pharisees (Mark 8). They discussed this among themselves, and with truly remarkable obtuseness decided it meant they had not brought enough bread with them on the trip. Jesus made a harsh but appropriate comment: "Are your minds still closed?" Even after his resurrection, he reproached the Eleven for being incredulous and stupid, says Mark 16. Now and again in the Gospels we hear of Jesus praising them; but much more often he scolds them; and the general impression is that he finds they do not and cannot rise to his greatness.

At least, this is the impression left by the first three Gospels. As we read, we wonder why it was necessary to report the blunders of the disciples and the rebukes of the teacher. For instance, why record the disgraceful fact that in Gethsemane, when Jesus was in a deathlike agony of spirit, his pupils *three times* failed to stay awake at his request? Would it not have been enough to describe his sufferings, with the sweat falling from his face like drops of blood, and to give the words of his prayer? Why should the disciples' negligence or disobedience be mentioned at all, when it could have been left in pitying silence? Sometimes indeed it seems as though the stupid acts and utterances of the pupils were described in order to show how far above them Jesus himself was. Thus, they thought it would be a nuisance for him to give his blessing to children (Mark 10:14); but he "was indignant, and said to them: 'Let the children come to me, . . . for the kingdom of God belongs to such as these.' "

The Gospel placed first, Matthew's, gives a truly dark picture of the pupils of Jesus. That named for Mark is scarcely any brighter—except for a short passage describing a successful mission, on which they preached and did miracles (6:7–13). In the Gospel of Luke there are two such missions, one by the Twelve (9:1–6) and the other by a group of seventy (10:1–20); and the disgraceful sleep of the disciples at Gethsemane is at least partly excused by the explanation that they were "worn out by grief"; yet even in the last chapter (24:25) Jesus is still scolding them for their stupidity.

However, the fourth Gospel, named after John, presents a far less deplorable picture. In it the disciples hardly ever get things wrong, and are seldom if ever reproached for dullness and lack of faith. When Jesus walks on the water, there is no mention of Peter's trying to do the same and failing. Whereas many of Jesus' early adherents are scandalized by one of his sermons and leave him, the Twelve stay with him, and Peter speaks out affirming their loyalty (6:59–69). After the Last Supper, Jesus and his pupils go out and enter a garden, but he is not described as praying there, nor do they fall asleep. And when he is arrested, they do not run away. Instead, Jesus himself says: "If I am the man you want, let these others go."

A new character appears in John's Gospel, although only toward the end. He is not named, but he must be one of the Twelve. He is termed "the disciple Jesus loved."* His influence on his master is exceptional—just

---

*Surely a very peculiar phrase. Did Jesus not love the other disciples?

the sort of thing which, in the other Gospels, sets the
Twelve to disputing with one another. Thus, at the Last
Supper, Jesus foretells that one of his pupils will betray
him. In the other three Gospels they all say: "Surely not
I!" or something of the kind. But here (John 13:22–23)
Peter—although usually so brash, so often the first to
rush into a difficult situation—does not speak directly to
his Lord, but nods to this disciple, X, saying: "Ask who
it is he means." Then later, after the arrest, when Jesus
is taken to the high priest's palace, he is followed by
Peter (as in the other narratives) and (only here) by "another disciple," possibly X himself. Only in this Gospel
is any one of the pupils of Jesus said to have been present
at the crucifixion. It is X; and to him, Jesus, speaking
from the cross, entrusts his mother.

After the resurrection, in the other three Gospels,
Jesus enjoins *all* the eleven surviving disciples to preach
and baptize; he names no names. But in the last chapter
of this book he singles out Peter for special praise and
responsibility: "Feed my lambs," he says. And "Feed my
sheep." The book closes with the claim that it was written by X, the special disciple "whom Jesus loved"—a
disciple who is not identified anywhere, and who, as far
as we can see, is not even mentioned in the other three
Gospels.

In the first three Gospels, then, the pupils of Jesus are
shown as being on the whole unworthy of him. He
knows it and says so ("O you of little faith!"). Often they
fail to understand him; and at the last they fail in loyalty
to him. Peter, the most energetic of the group, sometimes
gets things right, but more often gets things wrong. But
in the fourth Gospel the disciples behave much better;

and Peter, manifestly the noblest of them, is singled out by his master for special praise after the resurrection. As the book comes to an end, we find ourselves wishing to learn more about Peter, since the last words of Jesus, pointing toward the future, are addressed to him.

Why the difference between the three books and the one, when all tell roughly the same story?

Turn the page after the Gospel of John. The following book is the Acts of the Apostles. It begins on the very day of the ascension of Jesus into heaven, and carries straight on with the adventures of his pupils in preaching his message. Their leader is now Peter. In the first chapter he assumes authority over them, preaches a long sermon to a crowd in the second chapter, performs a miracle in the third, and is the spokesman for the followers of Jesus when interrogated by the high priest in the fourth and fifth chapters. After the death of the first martyr, Stephen, Peter continues to dominate the story until his imprisonment and miraculous escape in chapter twelve. At that point he quits the narrative. The rest of the book is devoted to the mission of Paul, preaching outside Judaea. The story carries him round the eastern Roman Empire to Rome, where it stops. It is a tale full of danger and suffering and death, but full also of miracles and growth and hope, and perfect confidence in the faith preached by its chief characters.

It would seem that the first three Gospels were written by men who knew much about the career of Jesus— either at first hand or by learning from first-hand witnesses. Everything was put down in these books, if it was remembered: even if it was an apparently unreasonable action, like Jesus' cursing a fig tree (Mark 11:12–14); even if it was a surprisingly harsh saying, like Jesus' declaration that any of his followers was as good as his own mother (Mark 3:31–35, Luke 8:19–21); even if it showed his pupils in a poor light or reflected his dissatisfaction with them. A central purpose of these Gospels was to describe Jesus' character and conduct exactly as they were, and to record his words exactly as spoken.

But when the fourth Gospel was being written (or completed) its author or authors had another purpose. The church that had been organized after the resurrection was growing in power and in prestige. Its first leader was Peter. He and the rest of the Eleven maintained it so well that God sent signs of His approval. Therefore, in telling the story of Jesus, the author of this book omitted most of the incidents and sayings which, in the other Gospels, sometimes make the disciples seem to be inadequate little men, who failed much of the time to understand their teacher and even to win his approval. And at the end of this book the author built up Simon called Peter as the successor personally appointed by Jesus, and destined to be the leader of the divinely favored church.

Thus, the first three Gospels are, in the main, convergent records of the career and teaching of Jesus. Their emphasis is on him as a unique being, scarcely comprehended even by those closest to him. But the book of John was composed (or edited) to bridge the gap between the first three Gospels and the Acts of the Apostles, and to show more clearly and convincingly how the church came into existence to carry on its master's work.

II

But the matter is more complicated.

The story told in the first three Gospels is related chiefly from the point of view of the Twelve. They were with Jesus throughout his ministry—except when he left them in order to be alone with God, to reflect and to pray, as after one of his miracles (Mark 6:46–47). Much of the story is divided between sermons and parables which they heard him utter in public and conversations which they had with him in private. So, on the Mount of Olives, Peter and James and John and Andrew questioned him *privately:* "Tell us, when will this happen?" (Mark 13:3–4). He always used parables in talking to the crowds, but *"when they were alone,* he explained everything to his pupils" (Mark 4:34). These and many similar passages sound as though one or more of the Twelve had memorized Jesus' words and actions and repeated them to others, who (or whose successors) eventually wrote them down.

However, there are some massively important events in which the Twelve took no part whatever. When Jesus was led off to execution, his cross was carried for him, not by one of his twelve pupils, but by someone never previously mentioned: Simon, a Jew from the old Greek colonial city of Cyrene in North Africa. After he died on the cross, his corpse would presumably have been taken down and thrown into some gully to rot. The Twelve, now Eleven, did nothing to save it; nor did the family of Jesus. But a rich Jew called Joseph, from the village of Arimathaea, obtained the Roman governor's permission to have it decently buried. We are told very little in the Gospels about this man, except that he was a secret follower of Jesus.

Jesus had other such followers, other such pupils. Some of them are not even named, and never appear directly. These are among the most mysterious and remarkable people in the narrative.

Two incidents stand out.

Jesus visited Jerusalem several times before the end which he foresaw. But just before Passover he determined to make a ceremonial entrance into the holy city, not on foot but riding. Neither he nor his twelve pupils owned any animal to ride on. From a stop outside Jerusalem he sent two of them to a nearby village. He told them they would find a colt tied up: they were to untie it and lead it back to him. If anyone questioned them or seemed to object, they were to say: "The Master needs it." They went to the village, found the colt, and gave the prescribed reply. They were allowed to take the animal without objection (Mark 11:1–7). A man in a village who owns a horse or donkey does not usually hand it over to total strangers. Evidently the owner already knew who Jesus was, and had been informed of his plans. *"The Master needs it."* The sentence sounds like a prearranged password.

Then again, how did Jesus and his pupils find a suitable place to celebrate Passover? As told in the Gospels, this is equally cryptic. He was staying in the village of Bethany, but intended to observe Passover in Jerusalem. Again he sent two of his pupils ahead. "Go into the city," he said. "You will be met by a man carrying a jar of water. Follow him. When he enters a house, go in and say to the owner: 'The Master needs a guest-room.' He will show you a large room, all ready and equipped." And so it happened (Mark 14:13–16).

Reading these stories, many people have assumed that they told of little miracles: that Jesus knew supernaturally that there would be an animal waiting for him to ride and a room prepared in which he could sup. Yet consider the man carrying the jar of water. Why did Jesus not simply tell his pupils to go to such and such a house and speak to the owner?* It looks as though he was already acquainted with the landlord of the house in Jerusalem, but did not wish to give the man's name to his pupils. He knew the villager who owned the donkey, but he did not identify him for the Twelve. Evidently Jesus had a clandestine organization of supporters who were all, or most of them, personally unknown to his closest pupils, such as Peter and James and John, who traveled everywhere with him. He kept the two groups separate: for, after all, was he not betrayed by one of the Twelve?

In the past fifty years we have learned much about the methods of underground organizations. Members of such a group never publicly meet one another or acknowledge its leadership openly. They commit little to writing, and send messages by word of mouth, often in cryptic forms. They continue their normal activities while working secretly to promote their cause. Sometimes they even seem to oppose their cause in public. They disclose their sympathies—if at all—only at vital moments such as a long-awaited victory or a crucial defeat such as the death of an all-important leader. Many men, threatened and pursued as Jesus and his pupils were, have been told to look for a guide carrying some simple but recognizable identification mark, and, without speaking to him, to follow him to a "safe house."†

---

*That is what he did in a simpler version of the story, Matthew 26:18.

†Did men usually fetch water? Was that normally not done by women, as in John 4:6–30?

Many men have been provided with transport and other necessities by a clandestine system if they gave the correct password. It is not strange that we are never told who owned the house where the Last Supper was held. The Twelve never knew his name.

In fact, Jesus had two groups of pupils. Peter was the head of the open group. It was Peter who risked his life by following Jesus into the high priest's palace. When Jesus said to him: "Before cockcrow tomorrow morning you will deny me three times," was this a prophecy, meaning that Peter would fail in loyalty like Judas? Or was it a command? If it was a command, then it meant: "Follow me and watch everything that happens, *even if* you have to pretend to be disloyal to me." No wonder that Peter wept so bitterly, if that was the hard but inevitable order he had fulfilled. From the outer room where the servants and junior officers sat round a brazier, he watched and listened to the interrogation of Jesus, so that he—the only one of the Twelve who had got close to it—could report what had been said and done.

The clandestine organization had, as its head, Joseph of Arimathaea, who adhered to Jesus "secretly, for fear of the Jews" (John 19:38). Close to him, perhaps equal to him but more carefully covered, was Nicodemus the Pharisee, who "went to Jesus at night" (John 3:1). Joseph must have been the leader, because he risked his social position and possibly his life, by "boldly" asking the Roman governor for the body of Jesus and giving it an honorable burial. He owned the tomb, hollowed out of solid rock and therefore expensive, but never yet used (Matthew 27:60). He wrapped the corpse in *fine linen* (Mark 15:46) while Nicodemus contributed *a hundred pounds* of fragrant spices to anoint it (John 19:39–40): generous, indeed lavish, gifts to the dead teacher.

To this same organization belonged the farmer who gave the donkey for Jesus to ride into Jerusalem. His name is not recorded; but he knew what he had to do. And then, who owned the olive grove called Gethsemane (the name in Aramaic means "oil press") in which Jesus spent the night of agony before his arrest? His name too is not recorded. Yet we are told that it was a favorite refuge where Jesus *often* went (John 18:1–2): therefore its owner must have been an admirer of Jesus, and not one of those who rejected him or plotted to destroy him.

In this clandestine group were many others. Nearly all remain unknown. They were quite unlike the Twelve; unlike also to the many overt admirers of Jesus who publicly gave him hospitality and were proud to have their names associated with him—for example, the little family of Mary and Martha and Lazarus in Bethany village (John 11) and Simon, the puritanical Pharisee, who invited Jesus to dinner and disapproved of the prostitute who offered him homage (Luke 7:36–50). Yet in the Gospels there are a few names that swim up out of secrecy: some personalities remembered although not fully understood.

The most remarkable is Simon the Cyrenian. He is never mentioned, except for one incident. When the Roman soldiers were taking Jesus out of the barracks (where they had humiliated him by staging his mock coronation) they compelled Simon to carry the cross. So say the authors of three Gospels; John alone asserts that Jesus carried his own cross (19:17). But why should the Roman soldiers pick out an ordinary Jew and compel him to take a prominent part in a formal execution? The Nazis used to pull in passers-by at random for questioning or for reprisal shootings; but the Romans of the early empire scarcely behaved like that, particularly in touchy and inflammable provinces such as Judaea. Why then did they arrest Simon and impose this hard and repulsive task upon him? Two little phrases suggest an answer. "As the soldiers came out," they met Simon (Matthew 27:32): therefore he was near the barracks. "They compelled Simon, who passed by on his way from the country" into Jerusalem (Mark 15:21, Luke 23:26). He looked like a countryman, just as Peter's accent had sounded countrified. Apparently the soldiers concluded that he was one of Jesus' adherents, watching the barracks, and so they arrested him and ordered him to help his master. A devout Jew unconnected with Jesus would never have complied: can we imagine one of the scribes, one of the Pharisees, who hated Jesus, carrying out such an order? But Simon obeyed. He too, it would seem, was a member of the organization, and was unknown to the Twelve except by name.

After Jesus died and was entombed, the Sabbath intervened. Early on the following day Mary of Magdala and other women went to the tomb. They found the heavy stone door open, and went in. The body of Jesus was gone. There was someone else there, someone whom the women did not know. Mark says it was a youth wearing a long white robe; Luke says it was two men in shining garments; Matthew says it was an angel of God, with a white robe and a face shining like lightning; John says it was two angels in white. (The Greek word *angelos* means simply "messenger.")

Here is an insoluble contradiction. If the being (whether one or two) was an immortal spirit of a higher order than humanity, then the removal of the body of

Jesus was carried out through the miraculous interven-
tion of God, like the Transfiguration. But if it was a man,
then he was a member of the same organization as Joseph
of Arimathaea. He was posted there to transmit a message to the women. Clearly he was expecting them. He
reassured them. "Do not be afraid. You are looking for
Jesus of Nazareth. He is risen. He is not here. Go and tell
his pupils, particularly Peter, that he is going to Galilee."
But the women (says Mark 16:8) were too astonished and
frightened to carry the message to the Eleven.

It would be valuable to know what happened to Joseph
of Arimathaea and Nicodemus and the others in later
days; but there is no reliable information. Some of them
may have joined the group led by the Eleven under Peter. Within a few days after the ascension Peter was
presiding over a meeting that numbered about a hundred and fifty (Acts 1:15). The clandestine organization
headed by Joseph of Arimathaea had presumably no further active functions to fulfill, and must have been dis-
solved.

Yet some traces of its work may still survive. As well
as the four regular Gospels which stand in the New
Testament, there are many other gospels, called apocryphal. As recently as 1945 one of these was found in upper
Egypt, written in Coptic, claiming to be the gospel according to Thomas and to contain *secret* sayings of Jesus.
Now, the words of Jesus as reported in these books sometimes coincide fairly closely with the canonical Gospels:
"a sower went out to sow," "if the blind lead the blind,"
and so forth. Sometimes they are painfully vague and
woolly, and look as though they had been invented by
some pious mystic who wanted to fill out the scanty

records of Jesus' teaching. But sometimes they are won-
derfully imaginative and irresistibly penetrating: they
have a ring like the actual voice of the master. "Cleave
the wood, and I am there; raise the stone, and you will
find me." Surely it is possible that sayings such as this
were spoken to Joseph of Arimathaea and members of
his group—out of hearing of the Twelve—and were
handed down thereafter to others who had never seen or
heard Jesus, but treasured what he had once said to the
pupils who visited him in secret.

INDEX